Journey Through Illness
&
Beyond

Brenda Shoshanna Lukeman, Ph. D.

Steppingstones Press

New York

Library of Congress Catalog Card Number: 94-066317
ISBN 0-9641416-1-2 (cloth)   ISBN 0-9641416-0-4 (pbk)

Steppingstones Press
7 Nassau Drive
Great Neck, NY 11021

This book is dedicated to all of the patients I have worked with over the years who, by their courage and struggles, have helped me to understand.

It is also dedicated to my dear friend Selwyn Mills who, through his valiant, shining spirit became, during his illness, a teacher of love and hope to us all.

I wish to offer special thanks and acknowledgments to the following people, without whom this book would never have been. My wonderful editor and encourager, Noah Taisan Lukeman; Adam Lukeman for his steadfast support and help with operations; Nick Curto, the cover designer; my copy-editor Anna Lapsansky; and a deep word of gratitude to my precious teacher Eido Roshi and dear Rabbi Ephraim Wolf.

This book is not intended to replace the need for professional guidance and care. It is a wonderful adjunct for the treatment that is most suitable for you.

CONTENTS

Foreword

Illness may rarely be easy, but perhaps it can be real. Perhaps friends, family and professionals who are willing to stand beside the patient can learn to become available to them in a way that brings peace and fulfillment to all.

This work explores the emotional and spiritual journey one takes through the process of illness. It explores the true nature of communication, giving, receiving and healing. It is based upon the premise that we cannot be of real help to another until we are familiar with our own emotions, needs and beliefs.

This work is therefore a journey; first, through the full spectrum of our own inner feelings, and then outside, to others, as we reach out to those in need of our care.

Above all, this is a practical book. It asks that we take our newfound understanding and apply it directly to our lives. Practical processes and exercises are provided throughout to help us do this. As we do these exercises, we are shown how to apply the material directly to situations in our own lives.

These exercises contain a balance of psychological and philosophical truths which help us understand and cope with issues that arise during illness and loss. They are derived both from traditional and contemporary modes of thought, with particular emphasis on the contributions of gestalt therapy and humanistic psychology. They are also wonderful tools for introspection and provide an opportunity for us to see the working of love in our lives.

As we become familiar and at home in our own inner landscape, we become more comfortable and effective in all situations we find ourselves in.

This is not a book to be read quickly, but rather to be experienced and worked with slowly, carefully and in-depth. It is a vital resource for people in the health care community and for those who are facing illness and loss in their personal lives.

Introduction

When someone we love dies, we die too. In our hearts there is no separation. And where are we now that a part of ourselves has vanished? What happens in the long passageway that many of us must walk between the time of a severe illness and our death?

This book is not about illness, but about the journey *through* illness to our essential health. Illness and health recur continuously, and yet we are not free to live fully until we finish dealing with our fear of loss. We are not free to love fully or to extend a truly helping hand until we are able to let go of that which we cherish the most.

Much of the time we live with the belief that all will stay just as it is. When illness comes we are shocked for a moment out of our stupor. We see that our time may not be endless and that *right now* we must say what has to be said, and do what has to be done.

Many, many questions arise in our minds when someone close to us is seriously ill. It takes a while to realize that these questions do not have one answer. They have many answers, appear in different forms, and may have different impacts on us at different times.

In a sense a finger is being pointed in our direction. These questions are demanding a response from us. We cannot be free from answering. Life itself is demanding a reply.

This book arises out of the deep need to find an answer to the following questions:

"How is suffering truly relieved?"

"What is the best way through serious illness and beyond?"

In order to answer these questions completely we need to understand illness in a larger context. We must also understand the true nature of suffering. There is no other way to find true peace of mind.

This book is dedicated to discovering the questions which need to be grappled with, learning how to look at them, and then starting to live from our own unique replies. It is dedicated to discovering the path of our own inner knowing.

During a time of crisis, we usually run in all directions, looking for help, trying to ease the pain we are feeling. But the deeper anguish of feeling helpless, of not understanding, is seldom looked at or addressed. The most basic questions of all are seldom asked out loud. However, they continue to rumble within us, beneath the surface, causing anxiety of all kinds.

"What is illness, anyway? Is it a random, senseless interruption of life, or only the beginning of new steps we must take?"

"Is my loved one going to die? What happens then?"

One minute the person was here, talking to us, and now he or she is gone. We are confounded, bewildered, lost and confused. Where has he gone? And what happens to those who are left behind? There is no other time in life more painful, and no other time when we feel more alone.

Often we run from the pain of this matter into forgetfulness. When pain comes we offer drugs. Instead of offering ourselves, we offer denial. We may not have ourselves to offer. Indeed, we are running away all the time only to avoid coming face to face with this matter. Only to hide from our real selves.

But if we stop running, even for a little while, we can see that the only true comfort will come from understanding, the only real healing will come from the truth. If we learn to listen closely, we will find that the pain itself has a meaning. It's there to be listened to.

"My friends, did you say you could not sleep last night?
The heat of the summer bothered you?
You could not find a cooler place?
Why does suffering have to come to us?
That question too, churned inside?
Wait, wait until the evening sun
Colors the mountain with its evening rays,

You'll get more than coolness the moment when
You answer that question, face to face."

Senzaki Roshi

We have so much fear about looking at illness and loss. We fear that if we face our suffering, it will make us feel small and helpless. Actually, the opposite is true. In this way we become alive and strong, reclaiming for ourselves the fullness of all our experiences.

This book is written by someone who is simply willing to consider this matter, and who has realized that this willingness is everything.

In this book you are also being asked for your willingness to stop running and to look inside. This itself is an act of tremendous courage, to consider these questions deeply, even though you do not know where they are leading you.

The entire book is constructed as a voyage, and each reader has his or her own particular journey to make. I appear as a fellow traveler, tossing questions and thoughts as if they were seeds into a garden. Some will grow and some will not.

Each reader, each person, is a unique garden, presenting a different kind of soil, a different condition of mind and heart, a different way of receiving the questions. This is especially wonderful. It is not necessary to relate to everything in the book. Certain parts will speak especially to you.

Simply put, this is a book of seeds, and you are needed to participate and receive whatever you are able, to absorb and let your garden grow in whatever way it will. All the answers to the questions, all the possible kinds of flowers that can grow in the garden, already exist within you. Only patience and care are needed for them to bloom.

This book is offered so that in the face of death we may become steady and simple and learn how to extend a truly helping hand.

CHAPTER ONE:
HEALING FROM WITHIN

"Things are not what they seem, nor are they otherwise."

Buddhist Sutra

Before we begin our journey through illness there is a fundamental assumption that must be questioned thoroughly. It is the idea that pain is terrible and must be avoided at all costs.

As soon as we start to feel pain or discomfort, we immediately try to stop it from happening. We look for some way to soothe or suppress what we are going through. We seldom stop and wonder specifically what the pain is saying to us.

It seems almost unthinkable to dialogue with our pain, to ask the fundamental question of it, "What do you want from me? And why are you here now?"

The Buddha has said that all life is suffering. This statement has been misunderstood in many ways. Many have thought it to be a negation of life. Just the opposite is true.

This statement simply suggests that by understanding the true nature of suffering and how to deal with it properly, we finally have the possibility of ending it, once and for all.

No matter what we are feeling there is only one pain and it manifests itself in various ways. If we do not address it in one mode, often it will come in another. It can come physically, mentally, emotionally, spiritually.

In whatever form this pain arises, it is extremely empowering to turn directly to our suffering and enter a dialogue with it. When we learn how to do this, we may even discover that the pain comes holding a gift in its hands.

When the Buddha became enlightened he announced that he was a doctor, bringing medicine to cure the ills of the world. What is the medicine the Buddha discovered, how can we use it, and what is the illness we are still suffering from?

Usually we expect the doctor to take control of our illness and make us well again. But this attitude itself is part of the original disease. From this point of view, we are relinquishing our part in the illness. We are denying the fact that it has come to us, and it is up to us to stop, listen, and discover the meaning and lessons the illness has to teach us.

Understanding Suffering

According to the Buddha, all pain comes from desire.

We long for something and cannot have it. Or, we have it for awhile and then immediately fear losing it. When we do inevitably lose it, we suffer the pain of loss and change.

We are always longing for and clinging to something. In the very midst of life, we are longing for more. As we finish one meal, we are already dreaming of the next. This kind of suffering, of insatiable hunger, is called the pain of affliction or greed. It is based upon the feeling that we can never be full and satisfied.

Or, perhaps we are longing for conditions to be different. In the midst of illness, we long for health. We refuse to accept our condition at the moment. Somehow we are not able to accept and experience each moment just as it is.

Modern medicine is based on the notion of battle. We battle germs and fight for life. But by simply removing symptoms something important may be suppressed.

We feel we must change life, overpower it with our own expertise. We have so many ideas about how everything in life must turn out for "Me". This may be called the pain of arrogance. And then, of course, life itself may not care about our particular plans.

The worst kind of pain is the pain which comes for no known reason. We do not know why it is arising and cannot grasp what it signifies. All human beings require meaning. We need to grasp what is happening to us. This

kind of suffering can be called the anguish of meaninglessness.

What has all this to do with the journey through
illness and the physical pain we have now? Some would
suggest there is no difference at all between our physical
pain, our illness, and the emotional, mental or spiritual
suffering we are going through.

PROCESS
**Think of three times in your life when you felt particularly
sad or upset. How did you handle it? Did you express it?
Did you take action upon it?**
What happened to you physically?
Take a moment and write this all down.

Illness often comes when we feel defeated and may
not want to struggle or live anymore. Some people become
ill when they are overly exhausted, which is a way of telling
themselves that it is time to make changes in their lives.
Each illness has its own story.

It is simply the same fundamental pain, manifesting
itself in different ways. Looking at one aspect of our
suffering, we also inevitably are looking at the next. All
aspects are interconnected.

When we are at the bed side of someone in physical
pain and we address the emotional, mental or spiritual

aspects, often the physical pain will startlingly subside. For full healing to take place in an individual, it may be essential for him to make changes in his total life.

Cancer can be suppressed for many years; and then it returns. When it reappears we must ask, "Why now? What is going on in my total life?"

"We become sick because we act in sickening ways."

Louis Jourard

We are reluctant to notice the quality of our lives moment by moment, day by day. We are all experts at brushing things under the carpet. Then the carpet begins to roll up at the corners, and we feel as if we are coming unglued.

During illness the body is rebelling. It is demanding that you pay attention to all that has been unattended. You may have been pushing yourself for too long. Now your body is fed up. Stop and listen to me, it is saying to you.

We could have been looking and listening all along, but we are not taught to stop and pay attention to and respect what we are feeling.

When we learn how to listen and how to reply, an entirely new life begins. Then the pain and illness become an opportunity for vital change.

Learning to Listen

Some say true listening can cure the patient. We usually listen only to part of ourselves. The rest is rejected. But no matter what we are rejecting, sooner or later we must come up against it, face to face.

For example, if we are sad for too long and have not done enough crying, our bodies may begin to cry for us through the illness we are having. If we feel that life is meaningless, our bodies can start to express this by shriveling up and dying. If we have held onto difficult attitudes, our bodies will bear the burden of them. Persistent negative attitudes become wounds upon our entire selves.

Usually when we feel pain our minds may tell us that something terrible is happening (whether it is or not). Here a negative attitude comes into play.

However, when we feel discomfort and tell ourselves that something beautiful may be happening, the pain will mean something else. Then we will react to our discomfort differently and receive it in a different way. We will not tighten so against it. This can be the start of an important change.

Many times it is not even the pain itself that is so terrible, but our thoughts about the pain. What we imagine within.

Throughout this entire book we will be looking at some of the attitudes we live with and take for granted as spiritual facts. As we look, we must bravely ask ourselves if these attitudes are conducive to health or if they contain the very seeds of discomfort.

The Path of Intuitive Knowing

In order to begin this kind of inquiry, we must examine the very way we know the world. Our usual way of learning and knowing the world is based upon being "objective". This is the "scientific premise". We take the world as our object, separate from us, something to be scrutinized and conquered by our understanding.

We observe, measure and define in order to gain mastery and control. All our faith lies in the rational mind and external senses. We feel that by thus molding the world, we are powerful, strong and in-command.

We spend most of our lives searching outside ourselves for things we already know. Running headlong to various disciplines such as psychology, theology and sociology, we hope that someone else will provide the answers for us and be able to be the authority in our lives.

We turn to priests, rabbis, and psychoanalysts and think that by mastering a new vocabulary we will understand something more deeply. We consider ourselves entirely blind. And in one sense it is so.

But after illness, death may come. When it does, it teaches us otherwise. There are many windows to view death through, but death is larger than all the windows. It cannot be measured, classified or contained.

The path of science is not a bad path. It has its function and great usefulness, but it is not the whole story. There are places into which it cannot go. It cannot bring us ease at the bed of a loved one who is suffering.

Where science ends, death begins. Death cannot be known through observation, as it has no form. Although we can prolong life, we cannot gain ultimate mastery and control over our ultimate destiny. When it comes time to pass, nothing can stop it. We are never separate from our dying; we always carry it right inside.

In order to gain true assurance and understanding at this juncture, we must simply enter a new realm of knowing. This is the path of *intuitive knowing*. This simply means stopping our search outside and beginning to look and to trust within.

This is the path of our own deep experience, a pursuit that will lead us not to *know* more, but to *be* more. *Intuitive knowing* does not talk to our brain, but to our entire being. It is the kind of knowing that can show us how to walk calmly into the sick room and stay close beside the patient with wisdom, strength and a real sense of beauty. It tells us that despite everything, all can be well.

In order to touch this possibility within ourselves it is necessary to ask new kinds of questions, to view the events in our lives with different eyes.

This book is dedicated to this new way of knowing. Throughout there are questions, discussions and exercises which will lead us on this different pathway. In this form of inquiry, we are simply directed to ask the *meaning* of what is happening to us. We do not try to mold or control our experience, nor do we try to explain it away. Instead we simply *meet with it*, become acquainted, and let it instruct us and be our guide.

In one sense, this is the path of humility. It requires the strength to let go of our need to control ourselves and our worlds. It requires the recognition that indeed we are not the most powerful; there is something larger than us, and we must simply learn how to connect with this in order to find our true source of wisdom.

Plato said that we are born knowing everything and that our lives simply consist of the process of forgetting. We have forgotten where we came from and where we are going. We have forgotten our purpose here on this beautiful earth. Now, looking within once again, we simply remember the knowledge which was always ours.

In the time of crisis, pain and sadness, it is of the utmost urgency to learn how to reconnect with our own inner source of beauty and strength.

This book is aimed at giving us the opportunity to see the workings of our own intuitive knowing. It is designed as a mirror to see into ourselves.

New Definitions

As we embark upon the path of intuitive knowing we start by looking at the ways in which we define that which is happening to us. Most of the time we react not just to events, but to the ways in which we have described them to ourselves.

Usually we think of loss or death as an enemy. But, how else may it be perceived? What is death, anyway?

From one point of view, death is simply the loss of perception of the familiar world. We like to feel that we are at home, secure and stable in the world. We aren't. We create many structures to give us a feeling of permanence and stability. Death takes them away, telling us that we are only transients here and this is not our real home at all. Where is our true home?

When someone we love dies, we die, too. It is not only their death; it is also our death that is happening. Suddenly we are brought to the precipice and may look into the vastness of space. We are thrown to the center and then we return.

We may feel discomforted, restless and sad. Our footing has slipped and fear can take over, creating anger and dismay. Despite all our protests and efforts, there is nothing more we can do. We feel helpless and out of control.

Loss is simply reminding us that we are not in charge of the universe after all. There is something else we must answer to. It forces us, despite our inertia, to look at the truth. *An opportunity has happened.* Our vistas have been expanded.

This does not have to be a grim moment. There are a wide number of ways we can respond.

Here are some different ways people have felt immediately after the passing of someone close to them, when they were facing the unknown:

"When my Aunt Sara died, I felt expanded, opened, sweeter, as though something lovely had happened to both of us. I left the hospital at about two in the morning and walked home alone in the city streets. A light snow was falling. I felt as though it was washing me."

"I walked out of the hospital and felt confused. Just confused. Where was my father now?"

"I still have Patty's stockings here with me. When we

were little, we used to run at the beach together. I still have her nail polish too. All along I had a sister. Do I still have a sister now?"

PROCESS
Make a list of the fundamental attitudes you have about life.
How do these affect your daily living?
What kind of toll are they taking on you?
What kind of health-giving attitudes could you replace them with?

Some believe that life is difficult, that we must suffer, struggle and have a hard time. Many pride themselves on this.

Nature does not struggle though. When spring comes, thousands of flowers just bloom naturally.

Some live with deep fear. They believe life is full of defeat. They never question these beliefs, but their pain and illness becomes testimony to what they are carrying around.

Some do not allow themselves too much beauty or pleasure. They drive themselves relentlessly. Is it any wonder they become so ill?

In order to deeply handle illness, it is essential to handle these secret patterns. For many people the word "accept" has bad connotations. It implies weakness and giving up. Nothing can be further from the truth. Acceptance is a vital act, full of strength and courage.

To accept means *to know something intimately, to become acquainted with it.* To accept means to *make friends* with the moment, with your experience, and not fight it or push it away. This leads to welcoming all existence, and true comfort in your life.

The value of welcoming suffering is that suddenly it is no longer external to you, an enemy to be fought off. You are not the victim of it or helpless because of it anymore. This attitude alone can make the suffering subside and transform in many ways.

During the practice of zen, we learn all about pain. Students engaged in zazen (zen meditation), sometimes sit for many hours on the cushion without moving. Sometimes incredible pain arises.

As they continue to do this practice, they gradually become stronger than the pain. They learn to see that most of the pain simply comes from resistance to what's going on. It comes from refusing *this very moment.*

When we stop fighting, we experience joy. Once we start fighting again, we are cramped into agony.

"It was evening of the third day of retreat. We had been sitting in meditation for seventeen hours a day. By now the pain was almost unbearable, and I was exhausted as well. I wanted to go home. My legs were aching and my back was stiff. Then it became time for the evening sitting. Three more hours to go. I didn't think I could make it.

"I sat down on my cushion and the bells rang out. After the bells, absolute silence. Soon the pain began to mount. There was no way at all I could escape it. The more I fought, the worse it became. Beside myself, I broke the silence and started sobbing loudly. I knew I was disturbing others, but I couldn't help it right then. The more I cried, the worse I felt too.

"Then, to my horror, the head monk shouted at me loudly, 'Shut up or get out. Go sit by yourself down at the lake. There is no pain. You are the pain. Become stronger than the pain.'

"At that moment I stopped struggling. The pain went. I went. Instead there was incredible joy."

Eshin

Being caught in an illness and filled with pain is like being caught in a situation we cannot get out of.

"The best way out is the way in."

Eido Roshi

The best way out is to make friends with the pain.

Fighting intensifies it. If we can relax into it for a little while and explore it, many new possibilities arise.

Natural healing is always available in all situations, but it can be cut off by fighting and by our fear. When we let go and enter the flow of things, we became available to our greater source of energy, guidance and help.

PROCESS

Lie down on the floor, take off your shoes and just feel whatever it is you are feeling. Gently become aware of whatever is going on inside.

Do not try to fix or change anything. Just take it in as it is. Where are you? How does the floor feel under you? How much space are you taking up?

Let your body react anyway it wants to. It can find its own way to become comfortable right now. (Get out of the way as much as possible.)

Now, you are making friends with all of yourself.

When you are ready, sit up slowly. (Notice what that feels like, too.)

Take a moment. Take another moment. All moments belong to you.

This attitude and process of making friends may be applied to anything that comes to you, including illness, disappointment and pain. Whatever happens, can you accept it for the moment? Can you find out about it and then allow it to go?

When you can do this, your illness does not become something foreign and frightening. You can live with it better, and also are better able to discover fine alternatives to it too.

To make friends with all of our experience, we need only become aware, moment by moment, of what we are feeling, doing and thinking about. We simply make a practice of saying "yes," to whatever comes to us.

Rejecting something over and over never makes it go away. In fact, it will come back time and again, just for you to accept it. Everything needs to be loved and accepted, including our illness and pain.

Health comes with learning how to say yes. Wellness emerges out of the balance and harmony of all parts of ourselves. It is the essence of reconciliation.

When we are well, we are in harmony with ourselves and the world we live in.

PROCESS
Look at your illness now. Do not run away from it.
Picture it within and give it some kind of shape.
What does it look like to you? Describe or draw it.
Now, look more deeply at what the image really means.
What is this image saying to you about yourself and the life

you are leading?

Listen carefully.

Next, ask the image any questions you may have and let it answer you. (Ask it what it wants from you and what it would need to go away.)

See if you can give it what it needs.

Then, picture the image thanking you and going on its way.

This exercise may seem simple, but it is very powerful and effective. It talks straight to the unconscious and puts us directly in touch with many feelings and thoughts that may not have been accessible before.

This exercise comes out of a meditative approach to our illness. The meditative approach enters its experience directly. It becomes one with whatever it encounters.

This approach dissolves the sense of being separate and alone. In this state of mind, nothing is our enemy. If something happens that is hurtful we still can understand it, and therefore it becomes our friend.

The meditative mind always allows experience to speak for itself. It allows life to arise as it wishes and respects whatever a person is feeling they need right now. Some say this is an attitude of true reverence for all life.

This attitude is not necessarily in conflict with medical treatment. It is not in conflict with anything. When medical treatment is required it is accepted like anything else.

The more a health care professional, family member, or friend can adopt this state of mind, the more they can help the patient to get in touch with what they truly needs.

Sometimes a patient may choose not to get well. This must be respected, too. We all have fixed notions about how patients should recover, about what kind of progress they should make.

But progress is different for different people. Some need to go through a time of great disrepair. Out of this chaos eventually new forms of life can appear. Sometimes we must fall apart in order to be able to start anew.

It is a great act of love and respect to give an individual the right to make their own choices, not just regarding the illness, but regarding their entire life. And to give ourselves this right as well.

Each moment we live in this manner, no matter how hard or strange the situation may be, we will find, oddly enough, that we are living in a moment of joy.

"Imperceptibly,
The green leaves lengthen,
Summer is near."

Shiki

CHAPTER TWO:
UNDERSTANDING CHANGE

"What do we have that we can lose?"

We come into life empty-handed and then expect to grab and hold onto everything. Immediately we make claims for ownership: *"This is my mother. She can't go away."*

Some enormous hunger begins to develop. What exactly are we hungering for? First it is only food and love that we are demanding. In the beginning it is easy to find satisfaction. But soon this craving grows more subtle. Our so-called needs become more intricate.

We want everything. We want to receive, to hold and possess. We want to have everything and to have it forever.

A little child in the store with his mother does not know where to look first. The child grabs whatever he sees. His toys belong only to him. His friends are his possessions also. The child insists they may not go away. This kind of attitude is hard to outgrow.

We feel we are the center of the universe and everything exists for our pleasure. We fight for our portion and then protect what we have with our very life.

When illness comes it is seen as a villain which is

taking our goodies away. But what do we own? In truth, what really belongs to us? Even our bodies have a life of their own.

The very process of our lives may be said to be a process of becoming hungry, searching for food, and then becoming hungry again. But we must stop to absorb and digest. We must be willing to discard the waste products.

We take in many goodies, but what are we willing to return to the universe? Certainly not those we love.

There are many kinds of foods we begin to require as we grow; emotional food, intellectual food, social food and spiritual food. The journey of our lives may be said to be the act of discovering the different kinds of food we need for our nourishment, how to take them, eat them, use them, digest and absorb them. And then, how to let them go. We could not live very long if we did not go to the bathroom.

Nobody likes to talk about the bathroom. But it is very important if we are going to talk about illness, about attachment and letting go. No one can live just eating forever. We must learn to be satisfied and to let go.

For many of us in this society our lives are centered around accumulation, around eating and growing fat. We become very proud of what we have accumulated; money, degrees, skills, friends, information, property, lovers, walls of paintings and photographs.

Soon we are full and overflowing. We are so full we can hardly move. Our homes are filled with possessions and we are still searching for something more. Most of our time is spent on hunting for the perfect object, job, or relationship.

It is not so easy to clean out the drawers. We have not yet learned the value of empty space. We may not have learned to make friends with our hunger and not let it be a devouring force.

Inevitably, along with the process of accumulation, the process of attachment appears. We become so afraid of losing that which we have accumulated. Everything seems precious, no matter what. There is little discrimination. We hold onto everything for old time's sake. Why?

Finding What Is Valuable

Why don't we stop and ask, "Is this valuable? Is this meaningful? Do I need or want this anymore?" Instead, we are driven to *do* more and *have* more and to feel that we are becoming bigger and better and wiser.

There is an overwhelming need to *become* something wonderful, to *do* something significant, to make our stay here meaningful. (As though we are not meaningful just as we are.) Here is an old zen story:

"A student was searching for a teacher to show him the best way to live. After many weeks of traveling on a high mountain, he came to an old Zen Master's hut. It was a simple hut, sparsely furnished and absolutely clean. The old teacher invited him in and asked him to have a cup of tea. The student waited patiently as the water boiled for the tea. Finally, when it was ready, the teacher prepared a fine cup of tea. The student held out his cup to receive it, and the teacher poured the tea. He continued to pour and pour even after the cup was full. Soon the hot tea spilled out over the edges, burning the student's hand. The student cried out in alarm. Why are you pouring hot tea over the edges like that? Just like this cup, the teacher replied, you are filled to the brim with yourself, your thoughts, feelings, and opinions. If you want to learn something from me, first you have to empty your cup."

The teacher in this little hut was asking the student to empty out his belief systems. Like this teacher, illness and loss help us to look at ourselves, stir our awareness, push us a little out of the sleep we are living in. We are simply being taught to loosen our grip.

Understanding Attachment

Why do we attach and cling so tenaciously? What

creates this kind of response? It seems so automatic, so natural and fundamental that we do not question it at all.

Attachment is usual, but not natural. Certainly, it is not necessary. It arises only out of our deep confusion about who we truly are, where we are and what is really going on. It arises out of a misunderstanding about the nature of our relationships and out of fear of being abandoned.

We feel the tighter we hold on, the less frightened we will be. The opposite is true. The gripping itself creates the fear.

Then one day illness comes to show us that no matter how hard we grab, we are grabbing only at the wind. There is really nothing we can hold onto, and the tighter our hold, the more we crush whatever it is in the palm of our hand.

We may not yet see we can never be abandoned.

This sense of crushing and being crushed is at the very core of the pain we experience. It is our resistance to the flow of life, and it is fed by the belief systems we hold on to so tenaciously. Many of us would rather die than scrutinize our belief systems carefully, or ever dream of letting them go.

Belief Systems

A belief system is a group of meanings that are created to interpret and handle the endless phenomena which addresses us daily. In a sense they are a particular window we look at our life through. Usually we do not perceive phenomena directly, but just our belief systems about them. Many belief systems have been created to make sense of that which we cannot understand.

Most of the time we absorb these belief systems unconsciously and carry them silently within, often not even knowing they are there. Then something happens and they erupt, often causing us much anguish and fear.

It is extremely important to examine what kind of belief systems we are living with, what kind of windows we choose to look at life through.

We may silently believe we are responsible for everything that happens. Then we feel like a failure if a loved one dies. This is an example of a belief system in operation. It is not necessarily the event itself which causes the trouble, but the beliefs and images we carry about it.

Since the beginning of time, belief systems have been created around the phenomena of illness and dying. Some say we are here only for a moment. Others say we are an eternal soul and come to this earth for a larger purpose— to serve God, perhaps, or redeem the world. For others death itself is truly nothing—darkness, loss, finality.

Here are some comments we hear frequently. What do these statements imply? What kind of beliefs are these individuals holding?

"What did he do to deserve this? He was a good man."

"She was so young. Why her? It's too horrible."

"If it was me, I'd give him some pills. Why not? What's the value of lingering in agony like this?"

"I saved and waited for my retirement. My wife and I made so many plans. Just one year ago, I retired. Now I have only two months left to go. What was it all for? Nothing. I feel as if I'm the victim of some horrible joke."

When asked specifically about their beliefs on passing, here are some answers individuals have given:

"I have come to do penance, to wipe out bad karma."

"Life is a purification. My pain will wipe all my debts away."

"I have come to learn lessons. When I learn them, it's over."

"Life is all a horrible joke. It's one time around, then you're over and out."

"There's no *purpose* to life. You live and you die. Only the strong survive."

"When I leave this lifetime, judgment awaits me. There is an accounting I will have to make."

"I am here only to learn how to love."

"I will return over and over again. There is plenty of time to grow."

"My spirit is immortal and will never die."

"Life is a pleasure, a blessing and a gift. I am here to enjoy it and say thank you."

For others there is even an alternative to physical death. These are the Immortalists who have devised a breathing therapy called *rebirthing,* in which they return to the time of their birth and release all negative thoughts and traumas which have led them to believe that it is not safe and pleasurable to be alive.

> "The idea that death is inevitable has killed more people than all other causes of death combined. It is certain that there are people living on this earth who are more than two hundred years old. All death is suicide. Your mind creates the death of your body. Your beliefs control your physical body. When you love your body as much as God loves your body, you can live forever."
>
> Leonard Orr and Babaji

Can you see how these different belief systems will create different reactions and actions during a time of crisis?

Deep into the night, when it's so hard to sleep, these

are the questions which may be stirring in one's mind. What will happen after this illness? Will I recover? What happens then?

It is the lack of knowing who we are and what our place is in the world that causes fear and trembling. For some, it may also be the fear that our lives and the way we have spent them may all have been some ridiculous joke. This is the pain of meaninglessness, which is the most painful of all.

PROCESS

Take a moment now to consider what your belief systems are.

How do you view your own coming and going?

Do these beliefs serve your life? Are they helpful to you?

Do they bring you compassion and strength?

Actually, the answers we find may be secondary. It is the examination which really matters, which really wakes us up. It is the process of examining our beliefs, feelings and automatic opinions which help us develop compassion and acceptance for other points of view.

When we become conscious and aware of our beliefs, then we have the ability to choose the manner in which we wish to relate to our world. Viewed in this manner, illness and loss are not necessarily a tragedy, but a *koan* life gives to us all.

A koan is a question given to a student by a Zen Master. It is a question that has no logical answer. It can never be solved by thinking about it. It cannot be known by searching far or wide. Yet, this question must be answered. It is a matter of your life.

Soon your koan begins to haunt you. It begins to ache inside. It wakes you up when you are sleeping. The Zen Master is waiting and you have no choice but to find the answer. There is nowhere you can hide.

Until life and death become your true koan, you do not really become complete. Unimportant matters become blown out of proportion. That which is precious is pushed aside. A koan restores everything to its proper order.

When you finally answer your koan, you become incapable of hate.

Let us now begin some exercises which will help broaden our comfort with life and loss.

PROCESSES WITH PARTNERS

Processes may be done alone by writing down your answers. However, if possible, it is better to share your answers with a partner. When working with a partner, do the process aloud.

First one partner completes the entire exercise (repeating

the sentence ten times). The other partner simply listens, offers no comment and says "thank you" after each sentence. Then the roles are switched. Each partner completes each sentence ten times.

When the entire process is completed, the partners then discuss their feelings and responses to the material that came up. (These instructions apply to all of the following processes included in the text.)

Say whatever comes into your mind quickly. Be spontaneous. There are no right or wrong answers. Whatever you see, whatever you feel is true for you.

You may answer the questions in a variety of ways: draw a picture if you like, write a poem, make a collage.

The art of these exercises lies in not judging yourself, not controlling or manipulating your answers, but in just allowing yourself to experience whatever responses occur naturally.

Do not be afraid of these exercises. Nothing bad can happen. If you begin to feel fear, just allow yourself to feel it, and then let it go. The less attention we give the fear, the less hold it has on us.

Work with kindness towards each other. It is always helpful to have fresh flowers in the room. After you are finished, it is wonderful to have cookies and tea.

Let us look at some images we carry about living and dying:

1. *To be dead is....*

Some sample responses:

    a. To be uncaring, not concerned with anyone around us.

    b. To be only in pain from morning to night.

    c. To be away from my mother.

    d. To be alone all the time.

    e. To be unable to say, "I love you".

    f. No pulse, heart beat, brain waves. It's simple. No big deal.

    g. There is no such thing as death. It's only a dream and I'm not afraid.

Now, draw your answer. Write a short poem about it. Take a piece of clay and construct it. Then change the shape as you wish it to be. Share it all with your partner.

2. *To be alive is....*

Some sample responses:

    a. To make love. That's it.

    b. To be ready to give of yourself completely.

    c. To be hard at work.

    d. To be close to the family.

    e. To go dancing and not sleep much.

    f. To watch the flowers come up in the spring.

3. *The truth about death for me is....*
4. *The truth about life for me is....*
5. *When I am dead I will be....*
6. *When I am alive I will be....*

Discuss the responses you had. Is death a condemning father (mother) for you? Is it welcoming? A friend? A monster? What would this imply about how you live your life?

How can you change your point of view to bring strength and peace to all?

CHAPTER THREE:
WHO AM I?

The sense that my world is stable and stationary, that death will never come, that I will go on in my present form, is the nature of all delusion. This kind of misunderstanding comes out of not really knowing who we are.

Most of us feel that we are our job, achievement, name or relationship. This is how we know ourselves. We identify with an object. We are this and not that. This group is good, the other is bad. There are boundaries everywhere, some strangers, some friends.

But like the object we identify with, we too can begin to grow static. We can easily become stuck in a pattern and unable to move or change. Somehow we do not identify ourselves with the basis of all life; that which is moving, changing and in constant flux.

> "Just simply alive,
> Both of us,
> I and the poppy."
>
> Shiki

The poppy is alive and blowing in the wind, but my static sense of identity is based upon a world that is stable and will not change. It certainly does not blow in the wind.

But we do change. We lose our possessions. Our husband or wife goes away. Our hair grows thinner. We try to pretend that this isn't happening and try to keep everything the same.

This very effort causes our suffering. We spend our whole life desperately trying to hold everything together and yet no matter how much we try, everything constantly falls apart.

Despite this, most people still feel that their security and identity can come only from holding on and keeping things intact.

Naturally, this false sense of security is constantly being threatened. It has to be. It is based upon that which is not true. At best it is only a holding action.

Then illness or loss comes suddenly and reminds us we are floating in the wild ocean, seated only in a cardboard boat. Is there a real ship we can board somewhere? Can we learn to become one with the ocean? Who are we anyway?

A very high percentage of men become ill and die shortly after their retirement. Here the sense of identity has been based upon the role they have assumed. Now that the role is gone, they are bewildered and disoriented.

"I was not sick for one day before my
retirement. Now this is my second heart
attack in a row. After I stopped working, I
fell apart. I felt lost. I didn't know what to
do with myself anymore. I felt there was
nothing I had left to contribute."

James Traubin, a retired executive

Role Playing

The job, the role, the family are all props that we live
with continuously. They are wonderful adjuncts to our
existence, but we must see beneath their function to the
very essence of who we truly are.

Many widows and widowers grow very ill and die
within a year of their mate's death. In part, this is through
identification with the mate. Again, the question arises,
who am I now that he is gone?

The very quality and direction of our life is based
upon our sense of who we are. The deeper this sense is
rooted, the richer and fuller our lives become.

During the Great Depression, many people jumped
from windows. Suddenly their money was gone. They
were their money. Who were they when their money was
gone? Nothing. So they jumped.

The anguish of being nothing, of having nothing, is

the most intense anguish of all. It is often not the physical illness and loss that is so painful, but the sense of not existing while living, of not being real, of being no one. It is the absolute despair of having no worth at all.

How is this counteracted? How do we know we are of value? Through what we have accomplished? Through our feelings? Through our actions? Through the loving eyes of another, knowing what we mean to them?

This is knowing ourselves from the outside in. This is wanting corroboration, affirmation, acknowledgment from the outside world. Our entire lives may thus be spent looking in the mirror of another's eyes. We often seek our identity through relationships.

We feel that we must earn our keep here and constantly prove we deserve it too. We do not see that we are already perfect, already beautiful, that we were born complete and whole. Nothing extra needs to be added.

> "All I ever wanted, mother, was for you to
> see me just as I was. I wanted to strip away
> all of the lies I had to tell you, all of the prizes
> I had to win. I wanted to stop running
> madly, living out your life for you. I wanted
> you to learn to be happy, and I wanted to
> learn it, too."
>
> Andrea, a 17 year old dying of Leukemia

PROCESS

Please answer the following questions:

How do you establish your sense of value?

What kind of image of yourself are you holding onto?

What can you lose and still be you?

What can you acquire and still be you?

How do you wish others to see you?

Sample responses:

What can you lose and still be you?

"My mother. My job. My teeth. My old clothes. Not my name."

What can you acquire and still be you?

"A car. A new house. Lots of flowers. A new boyfriend."

What kind of image of yourself are you holding onto?

"I have to be perfect all the time. I'm beautiful. I'm generous. I'm successful in everything I do."

Here is a young boy's answer:

> "stopping,
> and counting every sound,
> stopping
> and seeing every stone,
> stopping,
> and letting in the wind,
> stopping,

and not having to be somebody"
> Peter Rosengarden, an 11 year old boy

During illness and loss many feel as if they can no longer keep up different images. They are too vulnerable and changing too quickly. They feel they will not be pleasing and that others around them may take their love away.

The fear that we will lose the love we long for often makes us cling even harder. Or it can make others cling to us. But oddly enough, this clinging, demanding and sense of ownership causes more pain in the long run. It is often wrongly mistaken for love.

Over and over we say we love this person. And yet if the loved one becomes ill or changes in a way that is not to our liking, then our so-called love can easily turn to withdrawal or hate. We might even want to throw the person away completely.

What has all this got to do with really loving another? This is only a mirage of love, just a branch from the tree of attachment. It is possession masquerading as love—a counterfeit coin.

Dear Mother,

You feel you have a right to hold onto me this way, to demand everything. You feel we are bound together by some invisible bond that I, for one, never agreed to. In your mind we are welded together by an unspeakable tie. I do not want to be welded to you. I do not want you to miss me. I do not like the look in your eyes. It is harder and harder for me to have to pretend and say that I love you. If you really loved me, you would let me be. Please do not bring me any more candy.

PROCESS
Look at the ways in which you identify yourself and the demands
you make on another. Think of a person you care for greatly. Picture yourself with that person now.
With. . . . I am. . . .
Without. . . . I am. . . .
Pick someone else and repeat this exercise. Do it five or six times. Notice how your sense of identity changes with the different people you choose.

"Not knowing who we are, we cling to others."

Giving and Receiving

The very act of giving and receiving freely helps us let

go. But often we try to hold on by giving to others. Or we give to others to feel good about ourselves. Sometimes we give gifts that are too costly for us. This balance between true giving and receiving becomes vital during a time of loss.

What do you give others?

Some feel they must give to the patient constantly and are drained themselves, receiving nothing in return. For these individuals, here is a valuable question to consider:

What is the patient presently giving to you?

Often those who are ill feel so useless, so empty and so much of a burden. It is as though they have nothing to offer anymore. A deep sense of shame can pervade their lives.

Under these conditions it is easier to demand, manipulate and hold on, then to truly reach out and ask to receive. In order to be able to receive joyously, we must always be aware of what we are offering in return. This brings us a sense of value, a sense of being worthy of receiving.

Those who are ill are wonderful teachers, if we open our eyes and heart to learn from them. We might even ask the person directly what they feel they have to offer now. Discuss this openly. So much relief can come to everyone.

PROCESS

A wonderful way to go about this is to ask, "What kind of

gift do you want from me? Will you let me give it to you?"
Tell the person what he is giving you now. Tell him
truthfully.

When the giving is one-sided in an interaction, there
is a block to healthy flow. When we find that we cannot
give or take from another, then it is time to look at what
it is we are holding onto. Something destructive may be
going on under the guise of helping.

PROCESS
Right now, pick someone who is in the room with you and
give the person something that belongs to you.
(If you are alone, choose someone you know and write
down what you would give them on a piece of paper.)
What are you willing to give away?
What do you feel you have to hold onto?
What do you want back from that person?
Are you able to ask for it directly?
Sample responses:
What are you willing to give away?

"My handkerchief. Some money. I want to give you
my seashell necklace because I feel you are suffering so
much. A kiss. I'm afraid to give anything away."
What do you feel you have to hold onto?

"My pocketbook. Everything. My dreams. My mother and father. My self-respect."
What do you want back from that person?

"I want you to like me and think I'm nice. I want you to hold my hand tightly. I want all your money. I want praise."
What are you willing to ask for directly?

"It's very hard to ask for anything. I can't bring myself to ask for love. If you have to ask for it, it's not worth anything."

True giving and receiving are one. When we give fully without wanting anything in return, we receive as much as we give. Burden, resentment and clinging falls away. There is no giver or receiver here, only an open heart.

As we learn to engage in this kind of giving and receiving we begin to taste the fruit of real love. Real love makes no claims or demands. It gives the loved one freedom and space. It cannot be taken away, as it does not belong to anyone. It is always available and as plentiful as the air we breathe.

In order to taste this, we need only *let go* of that which we are holding onto, and become one with what is happening right now. Ultimately we will see that it is the very act of holding on that keeps all true nourishment away.

> "Dried salmon
> received, and oranges
> given in return."
>
> Shiki

CHAPTER FOUR:
BUILDING HEALTHY RELATIONSHIPS

Our entire life consists of building bridges. Each person we meet is another bridge, another link, a new way to deepen the love and understanding we can become capable of.

Especially during an illness the bridge between two people is the most important bridge of all. Yet, so few of us know how to build this. So few allow it. Or, if we do, it is only for a few precious moments and then we run away and hide.

In a sense, we are all like flowers longing for the light while we keep our petals closed. There is plenty of sun and light available, but if we are closed we cannot let it in.

The crucial bridge is the one which allows another person into our world. But there are many obstacles in crossing this bridge. Usually our first response to another person is to judge, reject, or make some kind of criticism.

We meet someone and immediately label them. Instead of being a person, they become an object to us, a client, stranger, or opponent. In this way we constantly separate ourselves. Then we wonder why we feel so alone.

Loneliness, separation and a deep sense of estrangement make up the real illness of our times. This illness becomes especially vivid during a time of physical illness and loss.

At this time when our need for real contact is most vital, instead we find withdrawal and lies. Withdrawal and falsity are so pervasive that they are even taken as the norm.

But during illness what is really needed most of all is to build a bridge of true communication. This rarely happens. So often we come away from one another filled with misunderstanding and confusion. Although we may not realize it, this kind of obstacle is simply a defense we have erected against being known.

Games We Play

> "Give up sirs, your proud airs, your many
> wishes, mannerisms and extravagant claims.
> They won't do you any good, sir! That's all
> I have to tell you."
>
> Lao Tse

In order to bridge the sometimes unbridgeable gap of loneliness we feel, we must also look closely at the roles we play—at the identities we cherish so much. These roles, dreams and images are often exactly what keep us safe and secure in our loneliness.

We wear many hats. In each hat we look and feel slightly different. These hats are comfortable. They ward off the wind, snow and rain.

But sometimes one hat gets stuck on your head. You don't remember that you have just put it on for the afternoon, and that your face is hidden underneath.

During a time of illness, or any time of crisis, the reality can be so frightening that immediately we dress up and begin to play our comfortable roles.

Roles can be hypnotic. We can fall in love with a role or fantasy and begin to believe it is who we truly are. Or, more commonly, we can fall in love with someone who is playing out a role. (Here we are not falling in love with the person, but with the image or fantasy they create for us).

It can come as quite a shock to us when the person drops this role and we are face to face with someone quite different.

Patients can easily become mesmerized by the role the physician is playing. It is easy to believe that this person is really in total command of the situation and even of the patient's life and death.

It may be comforting to feel that there is someone out there who knows everything, especially if we are ill and shaky. It can be reassuring to put ourselves at this person's mercy. Many people gladly give away their own independence of thought, relinquishing their decision-making ability in exchange for such powerful care.

Roles give us a sense of temporary security. Temporary security isn't bad, but it is only temporary and does not deal with the inner turbulence that may be going on. Sooner or later this turbulence emerges and can be destructive in various ways.

It is really much better to look a little more closely at the roles we are playing and the effects they have. All roles are based upon appearances, images and dreams. These images may tap into our secret longings, or even address unconscious parts of ourselves.

The biggest danger of being lost in role playing is that these roles may begin to play us, rather than vice versa. We can lose touch with the reality of what is going on now at this particular point in time. We can lose touch with our true responses and may not be able to see the wide range of possibilities available at this moment.

An incredible amount of misunderstanding and lack of communication comes about through being glued to a particular role. Unglue yourself a little. See if you can begin to separate yourself from the static role definition you have been living with.

Redefining Who We Are

A role is a set of behaviors intended to project a certain

kind of image to others and to ourselves. In each role we adopt certain behaviors, feelings and attitudes. These responses are built in automatically.

Within each role there are also forms of behaviors that we would consider out of order. For instance, we would be startled if our physician started to cry. Our physician would be startled too, and might even feel he was falling apart.

The physician might not be aware that his crying might very well be the best thing at the moment for his patient, and also for himself. But usually we do not consider behavior outside our role definitions as acceptable in any way.

PROCESS

What kind of behavior do you feel is off limits for you in the roles you have adopted?

How does this affect your overall functioning and spontaneity?

How does this possibly contribute to a sense of burn-out?

The limitations on acceptable behavior can cause an inner feeling of entrapment, burn-out and boredom that many professionals routinely feel. This kind of feeling comes upon us most frequently when our lives are mainly involved in performing gestures instead of acts.

Acts and Gestures

A gesture looks like an act. It is the outward expression of an act, but springs from a different source.

A gesture is not spontaneous. It is a proscribed part of an entire role. It is the "right and proper" thing to do—expected, regulated, predictable behavior. A gesture is the outward form. An act carries the inner meaning of the deed.

An act emerges differently. It is spontaneous, vital and completely corresponds to the moment it arises. It does not correspond necessarily to some pre-conceived idea of how we should behave.

All acts which arise out of the depth of our being are healing acts. They cannot be otherwise. When we perform an act as opposed to a gesture, we are speaking out from deep within ourselves. We feel as if the moment before us has been responded to completely.

This makes an impression on another person far beyond what we can imagine.

Being

We say that acts arise out of the depth of our Being. What does this mean? Existentialists speak a great deal about Being, about the deep, open flow of our existence, which cannot be limited or defined.

This natural flow which is available to everyone is often hampered and cut off. This happens when we live too much out of the fixed images created by our roles.

The natural, open flow of existence has no fixed roles. Everything moves, everything changes. We are here one moment and then there the next.

Most of us are afraid of this movement, so we live our lives predictably, encased within our set roles. We live more like machines than like true men and women. Then we feel stifled, lifeless and bored with each other and with ourselves.

> "A true man belongs to no time or place, but
> is the center of things. Where he is, there is
> nature."
>
> Emerson

For many of us the idea of being *true* has become confused with the idea of being selfish, not caring about the feelings of others. Oddly enough, just the opposite is so. When we are able to respond truly, enormous caring begins to arise.

Also, our way of Being strikes a deep chord with our friend. This chord reverberates in many ways and much of the estrangement we feel in relationships disappears all by itself.

On the other hand, when we act from our roles, we are implicitly demanding this kind of set response from the other as well. This kind of relating can be very deadening. Then we wonder why we feel so relieved when the other person goes away.

PROCESS
Look for a moment at what being "a true man/woman" means to you.

The way we act, the very nature of our responding, inevitably creates a response in the one we are with. For every role there is a complementary part the other must play in return. Just by virtue of the roles we choose, we create responses in those around us.

For every mother, there must be a child.

For every physician, there must be a patient.

For every tyrannical person, there must be someone wanting to be tyrannized.

PROCESS
What roles do you love to play? Take a look at the roles you play regularly. Write them down.
Which do you enjoy the most?

Which roles are you afraid to play?
Pick a role you like the best. Play it with a partner for a few minutes.
Now, reverse roles. Have your partner play your usual part.
How does it feel to be on the other end?

It is extremely refreshing and illuminating to take roles that are opposite to the ones we usually play. There is no better way of bridging gaps, acquiring understanding and relieving tension than by stepping into another's shoes. As we do this, our stereotyped images of the other cannot help but melt away.

All of this does not imply that we should never play roles. Life demands that we play many roles and versatility is required of us all. *The problem is not with playing a role, but with becoming so identified with our roles that we lose touch with who we truly are;* when we do not see that we always have the option of re-defining our roles at any time.

(Often a marriage will break up because the partners do not realize that it takes two players to keep a scene going. Each have the option of re-defining their roles and playing them differently, but they do not see this. They are so identified with the roles they are playing, they cannot break out of the patterns.)

Choosing Again

Roles are complementary. A role is defined by both individuals. Each person's part is inextricably interwoven with the other. The weaker I am, the stronger you seem.

The mother and child, the physician and patient, are dancing together. One leads and the other follows. But both have chosen to do the same dance.

You may choose if you want to play *the patient.* If you do, how exactly will you play this role? You do not have to play it as helpless and out of control. You do not have to demand constant attention. You may play this role in an entirely new way.

If one day you no longer want to do the tango, you may go and find a partner to do the waltz. There are an infinite number of dances to do, an infinite number of roles to choose from, and infinite ways to perform the roles you are in.

In the roles you are playing, it is crucial to ask yourself *who* has defined these roles in the first place? *Who* agrees to play them each day? What benefits are being received?

First we must realize we are not these roles. Roles are like a suit of clothing which we take on and off. We must take a good look at who we are without them.

PROCESS

Who are you? Describe yourself.

Who do you belong to?

What are you committed to?

How do you know who you are? Who told you?

Sample responses:

Who am I?

"Beautiful. Young. Slender. Kind. Smart."

"I'm a doctor. A mother. A sister. A rich man."

Who do you belong to?

"Myself. My family. My corporation. My church. To my country, naturally."

What are you committed to?

"Wealth. Pleasure. To working very hard."

"To my family. To my whole company. To working out."

How do you know who you are?

"I've won fourteen awards in just one year."

"By succeeding in my sport. By the money I earn."

"By the gifts my husband brings home for me."

Make a list of the major roles you play. How do you define and describe them?

What kinds of behaviors, attitudes and responses are expected from you?

Now, turn it around. Define the role in an entirely different manner.

Try it out. Find a partner and play it out with him.
Create scenes that will depict problems and personalities that are difficult for you.
Take turns playing different roles.
Play out scenes fully and discuss them.

Physicians and nurses in particular get caught up in rigid role definitions. This is also due in part to the strong expectations of them from their patients.

These rigid role definitions contribute significantly to the stress and burn out a medical staff may be subjected to.

PROCESS (For physicians and nurses)
(This process is described for physicians and nurses. It can be utilized by any individuals, occupying any other roles, too.)
Sit down and write out your description of your role as you see it.
Then, physicians should write out their description of a nurse's role.
Nurses should write their description of the physician's role.
Both should also include their description of the patient's role.
Now, form small groups and share your images and

descriptions with one another.
Notice what you expect from one another. Notice how
you do or do not receive just what you expect.

For example, doctors who see nurses as being warm and friendly will experience more warm and friendly nurses during their day. Often we elicit the responses we are expecting.

We constantly need to broaden our horizons. Sometimes the things we are most afraid of saying or doing are the things which will bring the greatest help, clarity and certainty. If we do not experiment, we can never be sure.

If we do not expand and grow, we begin to atrophy. Nothing can stay the same forever. By assuming new roles and looking carefully at the role definitions we have chosen, we begin to have a truly fresh sense of increased possibilities, flexibility and aliveness. This a sure fire cure for all forms of depression and burn-out.

CHAPTER FIVE:
STRAIGHT TALK

Communication is a massive topic. Basically, there is nothing but communication streaming around us endlessly. And yet most of us hear only noise without and within. The sounds of the world can assault, not befriend us. These noises can become so intense and brutal that our lives consist of more and more ways of shutting them down.

But living in a state of shut-upness brings neurosis and distortions of all kinds. Both emotional and physical symptoms develop routinely.

In order to set things right once again, we need only allow the world back in. When we stop labeling and judging each other, then the possibility of true communication begins. When we allow ourselves to receive the world's true communication then loneliness, confusion, and often even illness subside.

It has been said that if you can truly touch and be touched by another, then your sickness and pain cannot remain. It must become transformed instantly into the bridge that has been built from heart to heart.

"Just as the most eager speaking at one

another does not make for a conversation, so for true communication, no sound is necessary, not even a gesture."

Buber

What is communication? So much has been spoken and written on the topic that we may feel saturated even before we begin. Yet this is the essence of our existence; the need to be seen and known.

This need becomes stronger during a time of illness when we long to be in touch with others truthfully. We cannot continue our journey through illness until we understand different aspects of communication. Communication that brings health, that increases our pain, that destroys us in different ways.

Around some people plants grow wildly. Around others they wither and die. Why? Plants don't need a reason. They do not ask questions. They just bloom or die.

Like plants, despite all our reasons, we too just bloom or wither around different individuals. It is important to start noticing this. What is our visceral response? What do we need to feel healthy and whole?

Usually we are supposed to "like" someone because of his merits and "dislike" him because of his faults. But on a visceral level it often doesn't work that way. Deep down we love the so-called villains and don't really feel so good around the so-called saints. It is the fundamental communication that matters here, our visceral sense of what is going on.

Those who are ill are always in need of the kind of communication that makes plants grow wildly and makes us feel full inside.

Communication has many facets. We talk and listen in many different ways. First there are the words we speak. Then beneath the words, our body language. The subtle messages and movements we make. How are we standing, sitting, moving or gesturing? How are we dressed? What is our tone of voice like? Is all this congruent? Often not.

Many complain that they are not understood. Wives complain that husbands do not *communicate*. Nurses feel that doctors do not *communicate*. Patients often feel this way about medical staff.

Families, too, have their own intricate ways of communicating with each other. Some dedicate all their efforts to keeping each other from knowing the truth.

There are as many different ways of communicating as there are people, and just as many different ways of listening and being heard.

For some, their lives are dedicated to not communicating but to hiding, withholding and presenting a front. These individuals live in a prison of their own making. The unwillingness to communicate is a form of communication, too.

66

"There are no gifted and ungifted here, only those who give themselves and those who withhold."

Buber

But all pretenses are finally transparent. In one way or another we all see through the games that are being played. No matter how much we play act with one another, our deeper communications are always being heard. And they are always being responded to. It cannot be any other way.

PROCESS

When do you communicate most fully?
Who are you most willing to communicate with?
Who are you unwilling to communicate with?
Why? What's the difference between the two?
Notice how you feel in both these different cases.

Should I Tell the Patient the Truth?

Health care professionals, families and friends often ask if they should "tell the truth" to the person who is ill? This question itself is basically misdirected.

On some level everyone who is ill knows exactly what's going on. Some want to deal with it directly; others do not. If we listen carefully, and are respectful of the communication the sick person is making, we will see right away if they care to "discuss the truth" or not.

If the sick person himself is asking for information and we are reluctant to give it, please consider that the person is asking us for clarity of mind. Do we have a right to withhold it? Does this information belong to us?

Most of the time the fear about "telling the truth" is not fear for the other person, but for ourselves. The real question here is, "are we willing to openly face and deal with the truth?"

Look at yourself carefully. Are you willing to enter into an honest, open exchange? Or would you rather keep your distance. This is a choice you have to make.

Just think for a moment. Do you want to know the truth about your life situation? Are you protecting the other person because you would want to be protected someday? What is the value both of you could derive from dealing with this together truthfully? What are the difficulties?

Do not gloss over these questions in a hurried way. They are important, and there is no one right solution. Different situations require different responses.

Whatever choice you make be clear and honest with yourself. Either choice is acceptable, as long as it is made with awareness. What is not so acceptable is when we engage in *mystification*, either with ourselves or with another.

Mystification

Mystification is another form of communication. Unfortunately, it is too common around those who are ill. This term describes the conscious or unconscious efforts of one person to confuse, mystify, or deny the feelings and perceptions of another. This kind of communication obscures and clouds all well being. It is basically toxic and tears us down, including our will to get well.

The person who is being mystified has the sense of not having any solid ground to stand on. They may be receiving two different types of communication simultaneously. They may hear one thing with words and another thing non-verbally, or by opposing behavior.

The person receiving this kind of communication does not know which message to respond to. This kind of communication causes paralysis. It is the best way to drive someone crazy, including ourselves. Example:

Susan: "Mother, whenever I want to come close and touch you, you pull away.
Mother: "I do not. You're imagining it. Look, I'm standing right here."

Susan: "No, you're not. You're a thousand miles away from me."

Mother: "You are crazy. I'm right here. Look and see."

Susan: "I am looking. But I can't see."

What is happening here? Some reading this dialogue would immediately wish to deny or explain Susan's perceptions. That misses the point entirely.

Susan's feelings and perceptions must be accepted just as they are, although they may differ from what we see outside. Although her mother is standing at her bedside, Susan feels she is miles away. What Susan is asking for is inner contact. If her mother felt close to her, most likely Susan would feel it right away.

On the level of objective reality, her mother is there. Her body is present. But where is her mother really? Within herself she must be withholding the warmth and closeness Susan is crying out for.

The mother keeps pointing only to the level of objective reality. This is very confusing for Susan. When one is very ill, one becomes more attuned to one's own inner truth and needs.

Some psychologists would say that this child is experiencing feelings of separation and loneliness and then *projecting* them onto the mother.

The crucial word here is *projecting*. This implies that the child is simply placing her own inner world onto another. It does not include the fact that the child is responding to the inner world of the other person, too.

In truth, both activities are going on simultaneously. But for now, our necessary focus must be upon the ways in which the mother could be with the child so that feelings of loneliness and estrangement subside.

The mother might start by acknowledging that she probably is running away inside. She might say that seeing her child sick is very painful for her. If she could share this, the child would immediately be quite relieved and no longer feel so alone with her suffering.

In the dialogue, the mother simply became involved in defending herself. By defending herself, she was rejecting the child's feelings, not validating the child in any way.

If the mother would validate Susan's experience, no matter what the mother was feeling herself, this would give Susan exactly what she was asking for—a sense that someone was near to her inside.

When a person is very ill, they simply need you to honor them and their experience. And to honor your own. Or else they may feel quite lonely and alienated because they are having an experience which they feel no one can understand.

Being Real

Throughout most of our lives we all play a variation of the game "Let's Pretend". Let's pretend that you are King Arthur and I am the Queen. Let's pretend that you didn't say that and that I didn't hear it. Let's pretend it doesn't matter.

I help you keep your pretenses up and you help me keep up mine. In one way this makes us feel safe and secure. In another, it robs our true life from us. We begin to live in a make believe world. We become cardboard people, basically unreal. If someone knocks on our door to visit, often there is no one home.

When someone is ill and knocks on our door, they need a real person to be there. They want a real hand to hold on to.

When we live our lives presenting fronts to others, we lose touch with who we truly are. When our entire attention is riveted to the outside world, we become trapped in another's eyes. In this way, true communication is prevented.

When we retreat into roles and games the words we say will be empty. People will listen and not believe them. Our sense of trust and union will be impaired. When we are able to put our games aside, then true presence and love can arise.

Thus, the best preparation for being with those who are ill is working with ourselves, letting our masks go and becoming a real person. This may not be so easy at first.

Everyone fears being exposed. Some would rather die than have their masks taken off. Even many of those who are quite ill are still primarily concerned about how they look to others and the impression they will make.

Ultimately, illness and loss wipes out all images and takes away all masks and games. Who are we when our pretenses are gone? What is it we are so afraid of exposing? Why is true communication so hard to take?

PROCESS
Say "I love you" without using words.
Say "Go away" without using words.
Say one thing with words and the opposite with your body language.

Play with these exercises for awhile. It is very important to become aware of the discrepant communications we continually make. It affects the responses of others to us. It affects our own happiness.

PROCESS
Are you using communication to be in touch with the other, or are you using it to hide?

To confuse? To mystify?
What are you really doing, right now?
What is the underlying message you send?

We may communicate in order to express our feelings, to unburden ourselves. We may simply wish to deliver a message. There may be something specific we have to convey.

We may be communicating in order to influence the other, to control or elicit some kind of response. Example:

"You look so beautiful tonight."

How can you tell what is truly behind this communication?

The true intention here is not necessarily conveyed by the words. The same words can say so many different things. Some say we know our true intention in communicating by noticing the response we get back.

PROCESS

Find a partner and try out each of the following communications with him:

To express yourself.

To deliver a message.

To influence.

How do you feel in each instance?

How does the person you are communicating with feel?

Notice how they respond to you.

Contained in the way in which we speak to another is our entire relation to them. It may not be our words the person is responding to, but the way in which we view them. Implicitly, no matter what we are saying, we are always communicating what the other person means to us, who they are in our world.

The other person may mean nothing to us and we may speak to them as if they were an object, as if they were someone who existed only for our purposes, with no feelings of their own. This is a highly impersonal communication, delivered in an impersonal way. (Some may say "I love you" in just this way.)

In a situation like this the person spoken to will start to shrivel up inside. They will feel bossed, lectured at, or even pushed around. In severe cases, they may even start to feel as if all their aliveness was being drained away.

This kind of communication destroys life and enthusiasm. It does not produce health or joy. The person starts to feel as if they do not matter. And the truth is, in your world they do not.

Unfortunately, some patients have this kind of experience with medical staff. But a patient's own family members may also be treating them this way.

PROCESS

Talk to another as if they were a chair, only there to serve you or be pushed around.

Now, let yourself be talked to that way. How does it feel?

Say, "I love you" to a person in this manner.

Let them say it to you.

How does it feel? What kind of response do you really want to make to them now?

There is another way in which we can relate to another. In this way, we let ourselves be fully aware that the other is also a person. They have has the complete right to have feelings of their own.

This experience of the person makes room for their unique responses. We can allow the other person to be here as they truly are and not demand that they exist to suit our own purposes.

In this way of relating we are able to tolerate the other person's differences. We can give them all the time and space they need to express themselves in their own way. This kind of relationship can develop into dialogue.

In the first kind of relationship no real communication is possible. We are simply relating to the other as an object to fulfill our own desires.

In the second kind of relationship, we are opening ourselves up to something *other* than what we are. This can feel dangerous because it is unpredictable. We may feel as if something uncontrollable is about to take place. But what is possible under these conditions is the chance of a real meeting taking place.

Most of us create impossible standards for who and what we should be. As we do this work, however, false standards fall away and we become more in touch with the truth of our lives and more able to live it.

Indeed, we begin to see how much of a true friend we can be to others and to ourselves.

PROCESS

To whom are you willing to be a real friend? Why?
What is it about this person that you are willing to accept?
What about them do you find unacceptable?
What about yourself? What qualities are you willing to accept? What are the unacceptable parts, and what do you do with them? Is what you do effective?
Look at the war caused by these unacceptable parts that is going on inside of you. Is reconciliation possible?

Real Meetings

What is real meeting?

Sometimes we are courageous. We may allow life and people to be just as they are. We may even be very brave for a moment and allow our own heart to speak out all by itself.

Our hearts have a language of their own. The voice of the heart is always eager to be heard, though we usually try to keep it down. Sometimes it simply bursts forth. Then a real meeting can take place.

What is real meeting? How do we know when it is happening?

Real meeting takes us home to our center. There is no more wandering in confusion. We do not feel lost and alone. Our sense of alienation vanishes. We see that we are all truly one.

Real meetings can happen spontaneously. It can happen for a moment, or it can last awhile. It can happen between two people, or between a person and the sky. We cannot demand that a real meeting happen. But we can learn how to invite it in.

First we must see what is required for a real meeting to take place. The most important ingredients are two people who are real and who are willing to be here in the present moment.

This means that each person is willing, for the moment, to let go of their need to control the other and to use the other for their selfish ends.

It also requires that they forget about self-affirmation. They must forget, for that moment, about wanting praise in the other person's eyes or needing to be important, right, wonderful, or special in any way.

They are not using the relation to develop their fantasy. They are simply willing to be present each moment and to allow anything to happen, exactly as it wants to.

One simply has to *be*. To forget about fear and protecting oneself. One may even see that there is nothing to protect.

This kind of meeting is tremendously liberating. When it happens, some begin to laugh out loud or even cry.

Most of us have experienced a taste of this kind of meeting at one time or another. It is everyone's natural birthright.

In order to fully court this kind of interaction, we need to make ourselves ready. To invite it in. Some say it is as if we were preparing ourselves to meet with a great King.

Martin Buber describes this kind of meeting beautifully in his essay, "Between Man and Man." It involves two strangers who meet in the early evening on a deserted platform, waiting for a train. They know nothing of one another. One is reading his newspaper. The train arrives and the two enter the train, sit down together and do not speak.

Suddenly and unexpectedly, full communication streams from one person to the next. During this time each knows everything about the other. They feel as close to one another as to their very selves. Both hearts have opened and spoken, although not a word has been said.

Buber says it is as though a spell is lifted and the reserve which we usually hold over ourselves is released. This allows a true meeting to take place.

It is this kind of interaction which is most healing and satisfying when we are with people who are ill. Those who are ill are more ready for this. Being in crisis, they have less need to hold on. Their want is greater. Their time may be shorter. This is a very special opportunity for both of you.

To begin preparations for this kind of meeting, we must first look at what gets in our way. We must vividly see how our opinions, needs, judgments, falseness and intentions intrude upon the communication we make all day long.

PROCESS

Two partners are needed for this exercise: A and B.
The point of this exercise is to become conscious of what we are doing. First A communicates and B notices how he is feeling. Then the reverse. B does not make any actual responses during the exercise, just notices. (At the end of the exercise you may discuss how you were feeling.)

A communicate something to B as if he were completely unimportant to you.

A communicates to B with the intention of making him like you.

A communicate to B something that will seem strange and disturbing.

A should just be there with B. Experience whatever you are feeling inside. Then find some way to share it.

B's role in this is extremely important. What is required to really listen? What gets in the way? B should notice how much time he was really able to listen.

It is difficult to communicate when you do not feel anyone is listening to you, or when you feel the other person is sitting there judging everything you say.

Often when we listen we do not hear the other person, we only hear our own response to what is being said. Sometimes the other person only stirs up our own fantasies, and our fantasies get in between.

When you are listening, notice your response to the following questions:

Do you have feelings about what is being said? Are these feelings getting in the way?

Were you making judgments of the other person? Did these judgments get in the way?

Did you feel a compulsion to express your opinions? (This isn't listening. It's bulldozing.)

Did you want to impress the other with how silent and thoughtful you could be? (This isn't listening. It's making an impression.)

Can you release the person who is speaking from your need to have him be any particular way?

Is it even be possible that you could love this person, no matter what is being said?

It is rare and wonderful to have an experience of someone deeply listening to you, of really being heard. It is equally rare and wonderful to really hear what is being said.

As we prepare for a real meeting, we move into another level of communication. It is a level that is especially healing for individuals who are ill. Some call it communion. It is being in touch with that which is greater than us.

During communion, we are simply there, in the presence of another. Nothing extra has to be said or done. Instead, simply *be there*, open, accepting and fully available to whatever is happening, moment by moment. This will bring the deepest comfort to all concerned. Now true presence and love can arise.

"All I ever wanted from you, Mother, was for you to know me just as I was and to feel that I was wonderful. . . Even now, this very moment, I am still wanting it. Can you give it to me?"

Andrea

CHAPTER SIX:
INCLUDING THE FAMILY

When illness comes the entire family network starts hurting. Everyone in it becomes sensitized and in need of greater attention and care. However, the family is often pushed aside, viewed in annoyance rather than as an ally and valuable aid in the sick person's care.

Physicians, nurses, friends and lovers become possessive of their patients. The patient now belongs to them. Decisions about the patient are now in their keeping, they feel. They may wish to protect a patient from some imagined problem with a family member. Loyalty to the patient often includes keeping some part of the family away.

Rivalries now can begin to develop. Different people may begin to feel that their loved one is being taken away from them. They feel as if they are being replaced as the patient's primary caretaker. Lines of dependence are shifting. A great deal of anxiety can get stirred up.

However, the patient and their family are inextricably interconnected. When you touch one part, the other feels it. The needs, feelings and behaviors of the family members will inevitably have an effect upon the course of the patient's illness and recovery. Perhaps even upon his desire to live.

The whole constellation must be attended to. In order to do this effectively, it is very valuable to understand the kind of family dynamics that are going on.

What are the family members experiencing? Some react by becoming humble. Their endless pretensions are taken away. Often there is simply a blanket sense of sadness and free floating anxiety.

Sometimes a family member becomes intrusive and demanding. This is just their way of reaching out for the help and support they needs now. Or, at other times a family member may start to express the unconscious feelings of the patient.

"My sister is very ill. She's dying. It's not just her. It's me, too. I'm also very ill and dying whenever I look at her. I'm also facing all the fear and pain she is going through. Please realize, I need help too. I'm very frightened and now I have to be extra strong, extra giving. I have to be understanding of her, no matter what she says to me. I was never so understanding of her before. I'm trying my best, but there's nobody here being understanding of *me*."

Annette

The illness of one person can be a very difficult situation for some family members. There is a strong expectation now that the family will love, support and give to the patient in ways they were never able to before.

All attention is turned to the patient. The patient seems to be getting all of the love and care. This in itself can create a lot of jealousy and be difficult to bear.

"My brother can't come to see me anymore. He came in the beginning, but where is he now? He's out on the streets alone walking. I know it. He just doesn't feel he can give me all that love. He's hurting too much himself right now. I just wish I could see him so I could tell him I understand."

Andrea

It is unusual for a patient to have this much empathy. Instead, there is usually an implicit demand by the patient that other family members come through for them. This expectation arises not only in the patient, but in the other family members themselves. It is impossible not to be affected by it.

But a family member may not be able to come through for many reasons of their own. There may have been a difficult or ambivalent relationship in the past. Now suddenly this person is being called upon to give love that they just do not feel.

If they do not comply, not only is there guilt within,

but they may risk censure from the entire family as well. It is very important to bring this dynamic to light. Once it is looked at and discussed, a great deal of pressure may subside for all.

Undoing Guilt

Anything that helps dissolve the pressure of guilt is a crucial adjunct to health. Guilt is both lethal and powerful in the family during a time of illness and loss. Guilt itself can be considered to be a form of terminal illness that constantly erodes the quality of our lives.

Unfortunately, during a time of illness much of the interaction between family members may stem largely from guilt. There is the guilt that other family members are healthy, while this member is ill. A family member may also be feeling that the patient is now ill because they did not love them enough, or give adequately in the past.

Past difficulties in the relationship will now surface to be resolved. This in itself may be quite hard to handle.

The guilt is not one-sided. Patients may feel extremely guilty too. They may be feeling helpless, worthless and unable to contribute anything now. Some feel like a drain on the family and express a wish to be dead rather than feel this way.

All interaction that arises from guilt inevitably goes

the wrong way. It never produces the kind of satisfaction and comfort we are in real need of.

By opening the way for a family member (and patient) to become aware of, accept and even express their feelings, a great deal of good can be done. The patient or family member will no longer feel so alone. They will see that these feelings are natural and that they can be resolved. This, in itself, is very healing.

There is a wonderful process for a family to use to help dealing with guilt:

PROCESS
What have you not yet done for the patient that you feel you really should do?
Write it down. Make a list.
Now, write down what you think the patient would like you to do.
What would you really like to do?
Notice the differences and similarities between the three lists.
Now, go on. What has the patient not yet done for you that you still want him to do?
Write it down. Make a list.
Can you ask the patient for what you want?
Can you check with the patient about what their needs are?

Can you do for the patient what has to be done?
What is getting in the way? Are you at least willing to try?
Also, make a list of all the things you have done for the
patient.
Write down all the things the patient has done for you.

It is extremely moving and helpful to sit down with
the patient and discuss all of your lists. Accounts get
settled amidst laughter and tears. This process can also be
done by a patient who is experiencing guilt with a given
family member. The most helpful part, of course, is
opening all of this up for discussion with one another.
Tremendous relief and renewal is available here.

After this is done many have noticed that it is much
easier to do what remains to be done, and let go of that
which we are unable to do. We may often be surprised to
discover that the patient did not want it anyway.

Expressing Resentment Carefully

While guilt may be common in some cases, there may
be fury and resentment going on in others. In fact, much
of a patient's illness may be generated or fueled by this
unacknowledged resentment. Or by their inability to
express it directly.

A great deal of unresolved anger and animosity comes

out in a family during a time of a person's illness. In a situation of this type, a family member can become frightened by the illness. They may even feel that they have somehow hurt the patient and caused the pain.

In this instance they are really frightened of their own anger though he is not aware of it. These family members can become overly protective and worried about every little thing. They will not leave the hospital. They will not leave the patient alone. There may be considerable over-compensation taking place.

It feels unacceptable to us to express angry feelings or personal hurts to someone when they are ill. There is the implicit feeling that the patient is already suffering enough and can not handle anything else. Actually, a clear, honest expression of our feelings can work to relieve and soothe the patient in many ways.

Families often react by bottling up their feelings and trying to hide how upset they are. In the long run this is detrimental. It gives less and less reality to the relationship with the patient, creating only distance. The patient senses this happening and starts to feel abandoned.

It is healthy to allow, acknowledge and *carefully* express resentment or disappointment. There is no need to rant and rave, but to clearly, softly and honestly express what one is feeling. We can express our personal reactions without casting blame. It's not wise to say that "You did this to me. You're bad." That kind of communication is detrimental.

Just simply communicate what you are feeling now. Say, "This is how I am feeling now. This is what I'm thinking". One takes responsibility for one's own feelings and thoughts and does not imply that another caused you to feel these feelings.

No one causes you to feel what you feel. Things out there happen, and you can react to them in many different ways. You are not necessarily responsible for what has happened, but for how you are responding to it. And what you choose to do with it.

Relinquishing Blame

Family members (especially children) must be helped to see that their feelings did not injure their family member. The other person's illness is never created by them.

Most of the time we feel responsible for another's pain. This kind of discussion is heard frequently:

"If only we had changed doctors, this wouldn't have happened. He didn't do enough. I knew it all along, but I was afraid to take a stand against him. We all failed. It's as simple as that."

Family members, friends and lovers who are filled

with unacknowledged anger and self-blame often project these feelings onto the medical staff. They constantly find fault with everyone, and create a difficult atmosphere. These individuals simply must be helped to acknowledge and accept their own feelings.

In such a case, we may greatly help these individuals simply by telling them that they are not to blame for what is going on. It is surprising how much this may calm them down. Of course they may need to hear it over and over again.

A simple statement like the following can work wonders: "You must be feeling very worried about your brother/friend. Perhaps you feel you have not yet done all you could? Perhaps you are angry with yourself. This is perfectly normal. But it is not your fault."

Sometimes this kind of opening will help individuals express other feelings to you as well. Just your listening to and accepting their feelings will help relieve them of self-blame and guilt. It is not necessary to offer directives of any kind. Simply by being able to see that others accept them, a lot of tension dissipates.

Casting blame happens so often that it merits real examination. Often it grows into a gnawing guilt that persists for years on end. The deep sense of not having done enough, not having been able to save a loved one, leads many widows to die within a year of their husband's death. It also can lead to major, unnecessary surgery. We may not feel we deserve to live happily since our beloved is gone. Guilt after death is just overwhelming.

In the case of a child dying in the family, spouses usually blame each other. All the times they did not love enough now appear in front of their eyes to be reckoned with.

"I just couldn't look at my husband after Tommy was gone. I kept feeling he was blaming me, thinking if I had only been a better mother, more patient and caring, this never would have happened. I kept wondering if he thought Tommy might have wanted to die. Neither of us could part with what was left of his bicycle. Even though the other children desperately needed our family to remain together, my husband and I separated that year. We just couldn't take it."

Blame cries out to be looked at and understood as a perfect example of our own lack of comprehension of loss and misplaced sense of responsibility.

Families need to realize that they are not in control of the patient's life, illness or recovery. No matter how much they care for the patient, ultimately each person must answer for themselves.

Manipulation and Control

Unexpressed, unacknowledged anger that may be brewing within the patient and family can also manifest itself as manipulation and control.

There is no one as powerful as a sick person. The weaker and sicker we are, the more we can create feelings of guilt and obligation in those around us. We can make others feel they must monitor their feelings. What a tremendous trap this can be. This is most difficult to deal with because it is covert, subtle and can go unrecognized for long periods of time. It does not, however, go unfelt. It works intently, whether we know it or not.

Certain patients use their illness to get what they want. Their illness becomes a sudden opportunity for them to make all kinds of claims upon others, claims they may have had no right to make before. This kind of domination can be so overpowering that family members need protection from it.

A person may have been needy and hungry for a very long time. Now all of a sudden their illness gives them the right to let it all loose. Then family members can be overcome by the demands of this needy person.

A particular person may thus be deriving so many benefits and pleasures out of being ill that they can become unconsciously determined not to get well again. Why should they? What's in it for them?

Some patients become sick in order to "get back", to make someone else in the family pay. They may be saying implicitly, "Now you have to take care of me, whether you like it or not. You didn't love me enough before. You just have to love me now."

The price they pay for this kind of love is sickness and pain. Some pay it willingly. Unconsciously they are pleading, "I'll stay helpless and weak if only you'll give me your love."

Not too many family members are strong enough to remain unmoved by this kind of tyranny. Most feel trapped and begin to comply. They are not trapped by the patient really, but by their own feelings of guilt and fear.

In this case, complying with the demands of the patient can only make matters worse. When we give out of compulsion, the needs of the person to whom we are giving only intensify, and may seem insatiable to all.

As the person's insatiability grows, our own sense of inadequacy deepens. Nothing we give will ever be enough. The more we give in this manner, the unhappier we all become.

It is also possible that a family member may start enjoying the patient's illness, too. Be careful. Become aware. Perhaps the illness is making the healthy family member feel quite important and useful now. Or they may suddenly feel needed, where before they were not.

PROCESS
What do you feel you would be entitled to if you became sick that you are not entitled to now?
What are you willing to give another because the are sick that you are not willing to give them regularly?
Write down the answers as specifically as possible.

Sometimes a family member enjoys feeling stronger than the sick person in the family. Finally there may be some newfound power over the patient that they couldn't have before.

Illness can even bring a sense of security to someone in the family. Now the person knows that the patient won't go away.

In these various ways family members can become subtly afraid of the patient's recovery. All of this needs to be fully explored. How do we extricate ourselves from all these binds which we fall into? How do we determine what is reasonable, what giving is healthy and what is not? How do we come to realize how much we can give with comfort and ease? How do we learn to say *enough?*

Extricating Ourselves From Binds

First of all, in order to extricate ourselves from binds it is necessary to understand that if we are *giving at our own expense*, if we are suffering as a result of what we are giving, or if the person we are giving to is suffering, this may not be true giving at all. Eventually it will only backfire.

If we are giving (or being given to) out of fear, sadness, obligation, desperation, then that is exactly what the gift contains—fear, sadness, obligation, and desperation.

All we have to give to someone is our own state of being. The rest is superfluous. It is always only ourselves that we are giving.

If we come to one's bedside grim, exhausted and filled with a sense of obligation, then that is what we are giving. However, this resentment will not be present when you can say "no" comfortably, when you can find your own inner rhythm, find your own balance and determine what you can comfortably give.

Once this is done, give what you can gladly. You will feel wonderful. If the person wants more, you will be able to refuse them clear-mindedly.

Who have you refused lately? How did you feel? When do you plan to do it again?

Most of us get angry with others for wanting things from us because we feel we cannot say "no" to them. We feel we must give whatever is requested, no matter how outlandish, no matter what we have to give.

PROCESS

First look at yourself. How much do you feel you must give to another? (Pick an important person in your life. Then pick someone not so important.)

What is your cut off point?

What would you absolutely not do or give up for the other?

What kind of giving is easiest for you?

What kind of giving makes you feel replenished?

What kind of giving makes you feel ill?

Try to remember situations as examples.

What is it you most like to give?

Write this all down, and then share it with another.

If we go one step further, we will need a partner. One person is A, the other B.

A asks B for something.

B, can you give it? Do you want to?

A asks B for more. And more. And more.

A, see how much you are able to ask for, and how much you are entitled to receive.

B, see how much you are able and willing to give.

B, when can you say no? How do you feel when you say it?

Next, reverse roles. Then both partners discuss their feelings and what they learned about themselves.

It is important to see what is prompting our giving. Sometimes we have fantasies and feelings about what the patient is going through. We may be giving to another to allay our own fears. It may have nothing at all to do with what the other does or does not need. Please take some time and check this all out.

PROCESS

Imagine what the patient is now going through. Put yourself in his shoes and imagine what it is like to be him.
What do you think is going to happen to him?
Write about it, draw and discuss it.
Now, ask the person about his experience. How does it compare with your fantasies?

Sometimes we become so identified with a member of our family that we become confused about our differing responses and needs. We may have no real idea of what the other person wants. It may be impossible to realize that the person is truly different from ourselves. (Some do not even fully see that they are two different people.)

In these cases it is good to focus upon the ways in which one family member is different from the next. This gives everyone room to be themselves and have their own particular needs and responses.

So many of us are busy giving to the other that which we ourselves truly would like to receive. We can't give it to ourselves, but we can give it to another. Then we wait to get it back from them. We may end up waiting a very long time.

When we can give to ourselves directly, it is so much easier to give to the other clearly. It is hard to give of ourselves when we feel empty. When we give while feeling empty, the other person may feel they are robbing us. And in a way, it may be true.

Giving Each Other Room to Grow

When we are with a sick person we give them more than *our* presence—we give them *their* presence, too.

When we see someone as sick, weak and helpless, that is exactly how they begin to feel around us. The more sick the person seems to us, the worse they begin to feel. It is as though our very perception and image of them were being transmitted.

A sick person will find it harder to become well when those around him view him with dread and gloom. By relating primarily to the part of him that is ailing, we may be even suppressing his actual recovery. We may be ignoring the part of the individual that is healthy and strong.

PROCESS
Stop for a moment and try to see the person you are with as beautiful. Focus upon their good points and beauty. Now watch how they respond to you.

The more attention you give one aspect, the more it blooms under your eyes. When patients start to become well again, often it is because they become in touch with their natural desire to live and thrive. Just like sap in the trees, this healing force can rise in everyone.

By relating to that which is life-giving, you encourage the healing force to grow.

We must always be conscious of the kind of image we are perpetuating with a given person, particularly with someone who is ill. Your view of the other is always being communicated whether you want it to be or not.

Are you looking at the patient with disgust or pity? This must disempower him. Can you look through the eyes of strength and love? How you choose to perceive him is up to you. You can choose to see his courage, aliveness and ability to love rather than his weak spots.

The way in which you choose to see another person persistently will also inevitably effect how you see yourself.

PROCESS

Write down your description of the patient.

List whatever adjectives come to your mind. Are you focusing on his weaknesses or strengths?

Find five beautiful things about the patient exactly as he is now. Write them down. Share them with him.

Find five beautiful things about yourself, just exactly as you are now. Write them down. Share them with your friend.

Find five positive things about the situation you both are presently in. Write them down. Share them, too.

Seeing With Love

Seeing with love means relating to one's strong points. This strengthens, enables and sets them free. Seeing with love respects another's choices. Dependency holds a person too closely and causes weakness in many ways. There is a necessary time for weaning, the child from the mother and the mother from the child.

A good way to know if we are seeing with love and encouraging another to live and be well is to look at the effects our behavior is having upon the individual. Do they bloom a little around us?

It is also important to always ask ourselves if we are

giving to another in order to hold them or to help them grow.

When we truly love another, we also feel loved and complete. There is nothing the person has to do particularly to earn or deserve our love. We love and respect the person just because they exist.

PROCESS
Please stop and look at yourself for a moment.
What makes you feel most loved?
When do you feel unloved and ignored?
What helps you to feel your strongest?

The deepest act of love is to help others to love and value themselves. This is the ultimate way of extending an invitation to live and be well.

> "Real loves leaves no traces
> It touches and departs
> Just like an angel"

Eshin

CHAPTER SEVEN:
THE FINE ART OF PARTING

Saying Good-Bye

In the absolute sense, there is no parting. Yet we meet, touch and have to go. We then suffer so much, feeling that our loved ones are leaving and that we are ultimately alone. Deep chords of abandonment resonate within us.

Watching this happen, we may become grievous and sad. Sometimes grief is so overpowering that it is difficult to move on and try to love again.

When we are with a loved one who is very ill, we see only that which we are losing. We may not yet be able to see that which cannot be destroyed.

Fear can take over. We fear being close and may even think, "How can I bear to love you if I know that you may go away?" We fear really touching them. Closeness may seem like the greatest danger.

We erect so many walls for protection. But living our lives behind these walls we grow lonely and sad; parting, when it does come, hits us even harder. We missed the chance for the closeness we had.

"I was always afraid of my father, afraid to know who he really was. I was afraid to share my true feelings with him and let him know how much I cared. Then, one day, he was gone and I suddenly began to feel all the love for him I never expressed

"Maybe it was safer this way, easier to love him when he wasn't there. It's easier to love a memory, than a real person in the flesh and blood."

It may be said that we spend most of our lives retreating from love, holding back, waiting for the perfect moment or perfect person, or waiting for the other person to give to us first.

There is no perfect moment. This is the perfect moment. Every moment is the perfect moment, and every person is the perfect one. It's simply a matter of whether or not you are willing to love.

When our loved one is ill, it may seem too late to start sharing. We may not be used to behaving this way with them. We may even be afraid of the inevitable, having to say good-bye.

But until we can really say good-bye and be able to fully part from a person, we can never dare to love them completely. The dread of parting always hangs between us.

So, most of the time we are stuck in the middle,

holding onto the person for dear life, and yet holding back many things we feel and want to say.

When we learn to be with another without reservation, parting becomes simpler, more natural. We learn how to become complete. It is when we hold everything back, and have not lived out our time with them that we cannot bear to let them go.

Underneath this unwillingness to be open and complete with the person is fear, born of grief.

"When we parted
I thought the autumn
Would dissolve me completely
Even the old crows
Outside my window
Flew away haphazardly."

Eshin

Completing Our Relationships

In order to really say good-bye, we have to feel complete with the other. This means we have to feel as if we have done, and experienced with the other person all that was there for us to do.

We have to allow the other person to truly know us. And we have to truly know him, too. Then the relationship has been fulfilled. We have been the person we wanted to be.

Although we may miss the person, we will not mourn him so deeply. The person has become a part of us now; something vital has been integrated.

At first it may seem too frightening or overwhelming to complete a relationship with someone who is ill. You do not know where to begin. You worry about what their reaction may be. Also, you may feel a sense of futility that no matter what you say or do, it won't really change anything. They won't hear you. It's too late.

But it's never too late to complete a relationship. Just one moment of being present and truthful begins to dissolve much pain from the past. At every moment we have the opportunity to be the person we always wanted to be.

It does not matter if the other person does or does not hear you. Your own act of truthfulness releases you from a sense of pain and futility no matter what the reaction is. You have done what had to be done. You will feel different regardless of their response. And, in some subtle way, they will too. When you are able to do this with a loved one before they die, your process of mourning will be very different.

Where To Begin

Start simply by telling the other person what they have meant to you, what they gave you in your life. Tell what you wanted from them. Find the good things and discuss the problems, too.

It never helps to pretend that negative thoughts and feelings don't exist. The way you express them makes the difference. This is no time for harsh words or blame. Can you express your pain and disappointment responsibly? Not by blaming the other, but by simply stating how you feel?

When negative feelings and experiences are calmly brought to the surface, shared and understood, then we can be finished with them, and there is much more room available for our love to emerge. As this happens we see that anger and disappointment are only another part of love. You cannot have one without the other.

"Eve had been very ill for three months. Every morning I woke up and dreaded the day. All of my anger was like a huge wall between us. But I'd been angry with Eve for a long while anyway, and now that she was so sick I felt terrified of what I might do to her.

"So, finally one day I sat down near her and I just cried. I knew she was frightened, but I told her, 'I'm sorry Eve,

but I'm so angry with you. And I'm frightened too. Oh
God, I'm frightened.'
"To my amazement and relief she started crying too. It felt
so good, finally, both of us sharing a truthful moment.
Then I took her in my arms and hugged her. For the first
time then I could really hug her and tell her how much she
meant to me."

Mrs. Aubin, mother of a dying child

The very act of telling someone that we are angry or
frightened for them is an act of love and true appreciation.
The person knows it anyway. It is impossible not to be
moved when someone is being truthful with us without
being harsh. It is impossible then not to feel loved.

On the other hand, our falseness and lies are often
experienced as a kind of withdrawal. This withdrawal
itself contributes so much to the pain and loneliness we
feel. We think we are protecting each other by playing
some kind of game, but the numbness this creates is the
worst pain of all.

"The worst thing of all is to lay there and have them
come in and say platitudes to you that mean nothing at all.
They mean nothing to them either. You want to shout,
'Have a heart! I have feelings.' I want someone to come
close and tell me everything they really feel."

Peter, a 27 year old man with chronic heart disease

We will now do a process in order to practice and understand more fully what it means to be truthful and complete a relationship. As you do this process, old feelings of sadness, failure or anger may emerge. Do not be afraid of them. Let them emerge and let them go. This process is valuable, not only with people who are ill, but with everyone in our lives.

PROCESS

Have a friend read the following instructions to you:

Close your eyes, relax, become comfortable. You are now in a very beautiful place. Picture it. It is a place you feel safe, at home and comfortable in.

Now, picture someone you love who is ill before you. Bring them to you now. Think back over your time together.

What do you want to say to them? Can you say it now?

Let them answer you now. What does the person want to reply?

What is the most beautiful thing you remember between you?

Tell them. What is it that you would like to change? What are you still wanting from this person? What is there left for you to do?

Take a moment now and realize that the person is about

to leave you. What needs to happen between both of you in order for you to feel peaceful and complete? What has to happen in order for you to be able to let them go?

Can you let it happen? (If not, can you talk about it with them?)

Is there something you want the person to do or say to you in order for you to be able to let them go? Ask the person to say it to you.

Now, picture the person leaving. Picture yourself letting them go. How do you feel? What have they left with you? What have they taken away?

Perhaps you might like to make a drawing of this.

Underneath all of the pain, there is always love and forgiveness waiting. It may not seem that way momentarily, but inevitably it is so. However you cannot get to that until you experience what is in the way.

As soon as we have forgiven a person and received their forgiveness in return, all is settled and complete. Mourning is over. Only the love between us remains.

If we do not experience completion and forgiveness, we may spend many years occupied in grief after a person has gone. We are then simply holding on to anger and holding on to the person in a negative way.

PROCESS

Ask for forgiveness for whatever it is you think you did to hurt this person.

Offer them your forgiveness in return for whatever they may have done to hurt you.

The very act of forgiveness is so healing that often it goes a long way in restoring health.

PROCESS

In a case where it seems difficult to give or receive forgiveness the following is helpful:

List all of the lovely things the person ever did for you.

Make a conscious effort to find goodness in the person. (The goodness is there, and if you cannot find it, the block exists in you, not in the other one.)

Now, also find your own beauty and goodness. Make a list of all the lovely things you did for the person.

Tell the other person how happy and proud you are of him and of yourself. Congratulate each other.

(If the person is gone, you can do this in your mind.)

It is often so much easier to find fault and to hate and blame ourselves and each other. It is easy to forget or gloss over the fine things about each other and ourselves. This can be reversed consciously.

PROCESS

Dwell upon the ways in which you helped, loved, and cheered the other person.

What wonderful things can you do for him now?

Are you willing to do them?

Why not? (Does it feel better to stay locked up in revenge?)

Revenge inevitably backfires. When we are open and truthful with someone it is so much easier to let them go. And, although the other person may take his leave of us, the love stays with us and helps us to grow and move on.

"I always loved you, even before I knew you. Now that I have met you, I know that I met you only so I could see how much I loved you. This love was always there for you. Just knowing you for a little while, we have said everything already. My loss cannot take anything away. We are together for eternity."

Andrea, a letter to her boyfriend

Quality Time

When we see that death is approaching, time becomes new and precious. Time has always been precious, but we just never noticed it before. It is hard to waste time now.

The question of how much time is left can become an obsession. Yet, it is necessary to see clearly that it is not the length of time that matters but the quality of our days.

"My mother's pain came from many sources, but I have grown to see that it mostly came from her unfulfilled days, the dreams she never dared make real, from all the things she did not say."

When your time runs out, there is no sedation for this kind of pain. There is no way to recapture what is gone. But the possibility for change exists at every moment. While we are still here, life is beckoning.

The following is an excerpt from Andrea's journal:

"I didn't even know what it meant to be alive until they told me I was going to die. At first it meant nothing to me, nothing at all. The word had only a strange, hard ringing to it. Something about platelets and corpuscles and my mother crying, holding the bedpost. She just stood there stunned, holding on, and my father's head was hanging down. I just couldn't imagine not living and being here with them anymore. It took a lot of days for me to wonder about what it meant to be really alive and how much I had lived in my seventeen years. All of a sudden then, like a summer rainstorm, I wanted to live very much.

I wanted to run on the streets and taste all the ice cream cones quickly, before my summer ran out. I wanted to hug my mother and shake my father out of his stupor. Things I'd never thought of before. Things I had been afraid to do."

PROCESS

This is an exercise on guided meditation. It is best to do this process with a friend in the room. Let the friend guide you and read the instructions to you slowly, as you follow along with your eyes closed. It is helpful to play soft music in the background as the meditation goes along.

Close your eyes. Become as comfortable as you can. Imagine yourself on a road. The road is located in a beautiful place, somewhere that you have always loved.

Picture the road and the place carefully. You are walking slowly along. What kind of day is it? Feel the air. Look around you. Take your time.

Suddenly, up ahead, you see your death approaching.

Look at it. What does it look like? What is it doing? What does it want from you?

Speak to your death. Ask it where it is taking you. Ask it anything that may be important to you. Spend a little time in this conversation.

Now, you discover that you have about six months to live. You will not die now. Your death is fading.

Bring someone to you now, someone you want to be with. Who is it? Have the person sit beside you and talk to him or her. What do you want to say?

Remember the most meaningful thing about your life. Share it with the person. Think of something you would like to correct, or do over. Discuss that, too.

Now, think about the time you have remaining. How do you really want to spend that time? What is it you truly want to do?

Slowly, when you are ready, come back to the room. Feel the floor under your feet. Open your eyes. Give yourself whatever you need to integrate the experience.

Now, share it with your friend.

Dear Mother,

Even as I'm dying, I'm living. I know you won't understand that. I know you will still think I'm strange, and now that I look thin and yellow if you look at me from outside, I probably look quite ugly to you.

But from inside Mother I feel beautiful. I feel bigger and bigger every moment, as if I'm going to burst out of this body and enter into another skin. Soon the whole universe will be my body.

I'm living more, Mother, as I'm dying each day. I'm growing into something amazing. I wonder if you can understand.

If you can, please tell me so.

Excerpt from Andrea's journal

Journey Through Grief

The space between two periods in life (or between two lifetimes) is called the *Bardo*. It signifies a passageway, a period when we are neither here nor there.

During this period there is a sense of uncertainty about what will happen next. Often there is a sense of loss of moorings and some confusion and fear.

For many this period of transition is terrifying and must be avoided at all costs. But it is necessary and inevitable to go through transitions as we pass from one experience in life to the next.

When an individual is involved in mourning, he is in a *Bardo* period. To spend some time in this Bardo is both healthy and necessary.

It takes great courage to allow this journey. If we can go into it deeply, we will return larger and stronger than before we entered.

This time of passage, this Bardo is a gift and an offering. Many possibilities are contained within it. Here in the West we have little patience for time, process and transition. Everything here must be accomplished instantly. But the very nature of the Bardo, the very nature of mourning is that it takes its own time.

The fine art of parting is the art of knowing how to enter the Bardo, accept the grieving, recognize mourning and allowing it to end.

Both the Bardo and mourning are times of gestation. They cannot be rushed and pushed through. During this period we are being given the opportunity to die a little too. To let the outworn parts of ourselves vanish. Once they are gone, we can grow new and beautiful.

We are not sure we want to return new and beautiful. Mostly we just want to hold our act together. But at the time of grief and mourning, the more we try to hold our act together, the faster it falls apart.

There are many Bardo stages that appear during our lifetimes, many opportunities for transition and change. The time of mourning for a loved one is the most intense Bardo of all.

Unless it is entered into and completed, the grief remains and informs our lives in ways we are barely aware of.

Some mourners withdraw and will not go out anywhere during their mourning. We must not press them back to life prematurely. After going deeply into their sorrow and then returning, they will come back renewed and refreshed.

Many of us spend our lives in mourning, weighed

down by unconscious grief. We may even be grieving for the person long before they begin to leave. Our whole time together, our entire relationship, may be a defense against inevitable grief.

This is because we do not know how to be grateful for what we receive, and how to be willing to let it go.

In the Jewish religion, when someone dies prayers are repeated for one year. Basically, these are prayers of thankfulness, saying that life is good under all conditions, both when we receive and when we let go.

Moment after moment we must learn to say good-bye, to allow one thing to be over and allow the next to arise anew. Grief which will not pass is an attempt to hold everything static; it is a kind of cry against the very nature of the universe.

Incomplete grief can be a deadly weapon. It can work on us in subtle ways beneath the surface, dimming our pleasures, forbidding our success. It can be so deep and tenacious that it may even cause illness and death.

We may want to stop living. We may feel life is useless. We may be feeling very great rage at having been abandoned by our loved one. Enormous rage can turn into incomplete grief.

Many mourners die of a longing to be reunited with a loved one. This desire arises out of the sense that we are here and our loved one is somewhere else, apart from us.

We feel we can join them by dying ourselves. This is a very commonplace delusion. It can be quite vivid and compelling, too.

Incomplete grief can also make us hate ourselves deeply. Some begin to feel that their loved ones left because they were bad, or did not do enough to please them. Some feel that their thoughts of anger have caused the illness or death of their loved one.

Children often feel this way. It is crucial to discuss this with them openly, to help them make distinctions and clearly see that their feelings do not harm the other. Feelings come and feelings go.

When deep, irrational responses arise when a loved one becomes ill, anticipatory grief or mourning can be taking place. This is the experience of mourning even before the person is gone. It comes from the expectation of losing the one we love.

Some mourners do not eat or wash. Others seem disoriented for awhile. Do not press them to be otherwise. They may be in the Bardo. Usually these reactions are transitional.

Some may hurt themselves in various ways. There may be temporary desire for illness or punishment to alleviate the guilt. They want to suffer as their loved one suffered. This can be a way of staying close to the loved one, or of punishing them for going away.

Often there is tremendous guilt for just being alive and well while a loved one is suffering. We may then keep ourselves only half alive as an identification with the other, or as an act of penance. We are afraid to be too happy or well while the other is suffering.

These responses must be recognized and respected for what they are. Usually, they pass with time. If they do not, more understanding and discussion is needed.

It takes time to absorb the fact that a loved one is ill and may not recover, or may recover and be very different from before. It takes time to realize that we do not really help another by suffering with them, and that no matter what we do to protest it, some things are not going to change.

Some people see their loved ones in familiar places, others keep dwelling on memories. Some hold onto their belongings for a very long time.

This is not necessarily to be discouraged. It is simply the work of saying good-bye. We must be allowed to hold onto the person in whatever way, as long as we need to. When we are ready, we will let them go. Or, one day, we may begin to realize that the person has not left us at all. They will always be with us in all kinds of wonderful ways.

PROCESS

Think about a loved one you have lost. Do you presently

feel them with you? In what way?

Think of the people you feel truly close to. Where are they now? What makes you feel connected still?

If these people go away, do you feel less bonded?

Whether or not you are together, does this change the essential bond in any way?

Now, think of someone you do not feel so close to. If they are around a lot, do you feel closer?

What is it that keeps two people united?

There are some forms of incomplete parting that are harder to detect and handle. But these reactions may have unhappy consequences down the road and are equally harmful in the long run.

On the surface the individual looks fine. They go out all the time, running here and there. This may simply be a frantic need to replace the lost person, as if their survival depended upon the presence of another.

Relationships may be formed quickly and compulsively to fill the gap. But these new relationships often lack discrimination and care. They are informed by a quality of desperation. If the new person should leave, then all the incomplete mourning for the original loved one will suddenly surface in unexpected ways.

These individuals may be pushing away their experience of mourning by filling up each moment with frantic activity. Even though we may refuse to go through the grieving, it will return to us over and over until it is complete. The same situation may appear for us over and over until it has been thoroughly understood.

Most are terrified of real mourning. We are taught to be strong and dignified. There is the misguided idea that it is childish and weak to mourn so we desperately try to control our feelings.

This very effort itself causes the illness and constriction we feel. It causes us to run around frantically, searching for someone else to love.

It is healthy, courageous and strong to grieve. Until we grieve fully, we may not be able to really return back to life again.

If we want to help someone who is grieving, we must simply help them honor their feelings. Remember when you are with them that it is exhausting and sometimes humiliating to have to put up a cheerful front when you are hurting inside.

"I don't want to wear make-up now. I want to cover my face with ashes."
"All right."
"I don't want to go to my therapist now. He is frightened of me. He wants me to analyze my feelings. I won't."
"All right."

Grief is grief. There is nothing to analyze. It must be experienced and not excused.

"Bang the wall. Tell it everything you hate it for."
"I hate you! I hate you!"
"Tell the wall everything you regret."
"Can I do that really? Can you love me enough to let me be that ugly?"

We experience our pain as ugliness. It is not. Even though we are experiencing pain, we can be beautiful too.

> "I have always looked upon decay as being
> just as wonderful and rich an expression of
> growth as life."
>
> Henry Miller

Mourning ends when we are complete—when we have said, done and felt whatever is inside us. This may seem like an impossible task. It is not. As soon as we begin to do it, a wonderful process starts.

As soon as we feel complete about one thing, even one moment, we feel so wonderful that our mourning process begins to end right then and there.

The basic forces that keep mourning going are regret

and unfinished business.

Some have a sense that things are irrevocable and that they cannot go back and change the past. Whatever happened, it's too late. The damage has been done and cannot be repaired. This is incorrect. Everything can be repaired.

In fact, it is necessary that everything be repaired in one way or another. We may not be able to change something with a specific person who is ill or gone, but we can learn from what happened and then make the change (repair) the next time the situation comes around.

And it will. We are always being given opportunities to make things right.

PROCESS

Look at the person you are mourning for. What do you regret most about your relationship? (Make a list of all your regrets). How would you feel if this could be righted? What can you do now to make amends?

What amends did you make to the person while they were here? (Give yourself credit for it.)

As you do these processes, old feelings of sadness, failure, anger or pain may emerge. Do not be afraid of them. Let them emerge and then let them go.

Underneath all of the pain, there is always love and

forgiveness waiting. It may not seem that way momentarily but inevitably, it is so. You cannot get to that however, until you experience what is in the way.

As soon as we have forgiven a person and received their forgiveness in return, all is settled and complete. Mourning is over. Only the love between us remains.

If we do not experience completion and forgiveness, we may spend many years after a person has left us, occupied in grief. We are simply holding on to anger, holding on to the person in a negative way.

CHAPTER EIGHT:
HAVING THE COURAGE TO MOVE ON

"The world is a womb, not a tomb, a place
where everything is engendered and brought
to life."

Henry Miller

An Invitation To Live Again

Just as we must learn to part, we must also learn how
to be born and move on. We must learn how to open our
hearts and to grow constantly. To grow one inch is not
enough.

Most of us live this incredible life half asleep, walking
around in a dream. What a waste! This life is such a
miraculous gift which most of us refuse day after day.

Why do we consistently refuse to taste so much
beauty and joy? And what must we do to let it all in?

First we must learn to throw everything we have to the
wind, and let the wind bring back to us whatever it wants
to, whenever it wants. We limit ourselves because we are
so busy holding on to so many ideas of what life "should"
bring us—what we expect and demand. This very holding
on keeps us from living, tasting life and falling in love over

and over again.

To live fully requires courage and faith. We hear a great deal about the word faith, but how can we make it real in our lives? Although there are many beliefs we carry about faith, it is rare to see a person with true faith in life itself. Or true faith in their own experiences.

Most of the time we feel bewildered by events and spend most of our lives trying to change them or make them go away. A great deal of energy and thought is spent trying to shape our days to our particular wishes. Why do we think we know what is best?

When events do not go as we planned we become fearful and sad. Some become desperate and say life has lost its purpose and that they have lost their direction. They may not yet have seen that all directions have the same destination, and that whether we know it or not, this destination is wonderful.

> "Walk to the left,
> Walk to the right,
> But above all
> Don't fall down."
>
> Zen saying

It's all right to fall down. We can get up again. It can even be fun to lose our direction, though we've been taught to be cautious and hesitate. Yet the more we hesitate the more wobbly and afraid we become. We must finally stop wobbling and walk with faith wherever life is taking us.

Faith implies taking a leap. It means being willing to stand up and walk bravely in spite of all that we do not know. It means trusting ourselves even though we are erratic, and accepting that life is fundamentally good and that we are always in good hands, whether it seems that way or not.

When we are good, life is good. When we are upset, life is terrifying.

We think strength consists of holding on to old ideas and forms. But new life always comes with the dissolution of the old. Without letting go, nothing new can appear. Waste products become fertilizers for the soil much the way old ideas and ways become fertilizers for our new growth. It is all part of one circle. We must allow the old to dissolve in order to fertilize the new.

All that is formed is subject to change. It cannot be any other way. One day we may even see for ourselves that we are part of a formation, a coming together and falling away. Nothing is constant and everything is constant, and this exists simultaneously.

Change itself is constant, and our particular lives change constantly. Death is only another part of the cycle of life. This is difficult for us to accept. We may want to protest and go on marches. But who are we to give orders? Why can't we allow the universe to be as it is?

If we love and do not interfere with the universe, then it will replenish us constantly because it is in its nature to do so. Just look at the earth in spring.

> "The plum tree of my hut,
> It couldn't be helped,
> It bloomed."
>
> Shiki

We may not feel as if we deserve to bloom and constantly be replenished. We have been taught to condemn who we are. This deep self condemnation must be uprooted. It is such a strong factor in causing illness. Some say it is the illness itself.

Being Born

A book about illness inevitably has to be a book about birth, too. Illness is an opportunity for us to know the fullness of our entire selves.

Most of us think we are stuck with ourselves forever and have to be the way we are. Others feel they have to literally die in order to start all over again.

But, you can start all over again right now. You must

simply be willing to allow the possibilities within you to appear. It's like having a room and changing the furniture. First, spring cleaning, then new colors and pieces, one piece at a time.

PROCESS

Now, let us look at our own life process, at our own need to be born. Find a partner and share it with him.

Each partner completes the following sentence spontaneously several times. The other listens and says "thank you."

Then reverse.

To be really alive is....

The part of me that is really alive is....

The part of me that is most dead is....

The part of me that wants to be born is....

PROCESS

This is a guided meditation that will help you see parts of yourself that want to be born and parts that want to go away. You will need a partner to read the instructions carefully to you. Some enjoy having soft music in the background.

Close your eyes, relax and become at ease. Now, picture yourself in a place you love to be where you feel safe and happy. Look at the place closely. How do you feel now?

Now, get an image of the part of yourself that you would like to be born. (If you like, you may see him coming down the road.)

What is he like? Look at him closely. Make friends. What is his name? What does he do? What kinds of songs does he like to sing?

Is there something he wants to say to you? Is there something you may want to reply? Is there some particular person that he wants nearby?

Now, ask yourself, what is in the way of this person being born?

Get another image as an answer to the question. See what this image means. Talk to it and let it answer. Ask what it is afraid of and what is required in order for it to let the obstacle go away.

See if you can give it to him. Be very gentle with yourself. You are not going to obliterate the obstacle; you are simply going to let it go away.

When you are ready open your eyes, come back to the room and either draw a picture of the journey you've made or share it with your partner when you wish to.

If you care to, you can play act being the new person. Introduce yourself as the new person to your partner. Get a real feeling of what it is like to be him.

This process is very enjoyable and illuminating. It can quickly bring us in touch with the endless possibilities that always exist within us for new experiences and expression.

When we really see how much we contain within, we see that we never have to grow stale and die. Dying may be here just to remind us that sometimes we have no choice but to let go and be born again.

Finding Forever

"But I want my mommy to stay with me forever."

"What is forever, Pamela?"

"I don't know. I read about it in a book somewhere."

"What does forever look like, Pamela?"

(smiling a little) "Maybe my freckles will last forever?"

"Can you draw me a picture of forever?"

"This is silly, but I'll draw it anyway."

"And what happens when forever goes away?"

Pamela, a nine year old cancer patient

It is very helpful to become clear and concrete about the concept of forever, which somehow walls us in. We have a strong sense of things lasting forever. But what is forever? Can we taste it? Touch it? How do we really know about forever? It is only a figment of our imagination. Once we begin to examine this closely the fearful aspects of the concept dissolve spontaneously.

PROCESS
What is forever?
Look at this very specifically. Make a drawing or shape it with clay.
How do you interact with forever during your life, day by day?

Particularly during a time of illness and loss, we begin to search for something which is stable, which will not alter or go away.

What is it that does not change or go away?

Examine this closely. Some will say that God does not alter. God is eternal. Then it is necessary to find God for ourselves, moment by moment in the middle of the flux.

It is necessary to take the Eternal with you directly back to the sick bed. How do you do that? Just a concept is not enough. It does not bring ease when we are in pain. At this time it is necessary to make the concept concrete, vivid and thoroughly real.

"Painted cakes do not satisfy hunger."

PROCESS
If you want to find God, where do you look for Him?
"He sleeps next to my mother's bed."

"In the rainbow."
"When it snows, I see God's face smiling."
"In chocolate chip ice-cream cones."

During a time of serious illness, many begin to think about God. Some feel ashamed and uncomfortable just to talk about it out loud. They feel that by now they should have outgrown such foolishness. Others carry a secret longing to feel God's presence with them.

It is enormously helpful to discuss this openly. It doesn't matter what one's beliefs are. Just to open this up for discussion relieves a great deal of tension and stress.

Mrs. Adams: (laughing, slightly embarrassed) Well, of course I haven't talked, or really thought about God since I was a child. We outgrow that kind of thing. I did go to church occasionally, but, well, I didn't discuss it much. Recently, all of this has been with me again. It's nice of you to ask.

Often, all that is needed to open up this area is to gently remark, "I sometimes think about God, do you?"

It is then amazing to see how a patient, friend, or relative will begin to pour out their thoughts, fears and desires.

Now it is particularly important to be entirely open to

the feelings of the other and not to offer your own point of view. Your point of view is your own and not necessarily relevant to the journey the other person is on.

At this time it is most helpful to offer an open, accepting attitude so that the patient, friend or relative is free to explore what is true for them.

Just the freedom in being listened to, not judged, not taught, just really listened to, is tremendously healing in itself.

The search for God, meaning or eternity is another form of the search for ourselves.

Prayer

It is impossible to write a book on illness without talking about prayer. Very few of us know what prayer really is, or dream of taking it seriously. Actually, prayer is the fulfillment of man's development.

However, for many, prayer is simply a repetition of old, childlike behavior, mainly inspired by fear. In our society it is mostly considered superstitious and irrational, done mainly out of rote.

Most of us think prayer is "asking for something". But this is not necessarily true. It is true that prayers are commonly offered for long life, health, wealth, happiness, and so on. This comes from feeling needful and empty.

This kind of prayer is not an overflowing, which comes from feeling full.

Some offer prayers for repentance, arising out of deep feelings of guilt. These are the prayers that are asking that we be cleansed of our sins.

Some make offerings. Others feel that to pray is to give a gift. For some, prayer means chanting; for others, singing, meditating, dancing, bowing or working with love in their own garden.

Prayer is its own answer. Inevitably an answer will come, one way or another. But often not in the way you imagined.

True prayer is an activity through which man reaches for the highest in himself and allows his separateness to fall away. Prayer is the very door to our center. It is the key that unlocks our heart.

It is the very process of becoming one with all beings, and of regarding them with reverence and awe. It is also a way of being in the world.

Prayer is a natural human function that has been severely repressed and distorted for many. From a psychological point of view, prayer has a natural healing power. It has an expanding, soothing, clarifying effect.

Just as it is natural for the human being to seek friendship, it is natural for the human being to turn towards prayer.

During a time of illness, it is extremely beneficial to turn toward prayer, to turn towards our larger being and establish communication. In the state of prayer we are relating o urselves t o something larger than our own personal selves. We may also be inviting this larger sense of life to permeate our entire being in all kinds of ways.

The mind of prayer is a mind that is giving thanks for the gift of life and is willing to celebrate it continually. It is a state of mind that beautifies its surroundings wherever it goes.

The Banquet Of Life

Prayer becomes very, very necessary because it is easy for us to forget. Many of us live our lives like ungrateful guests at the marvelous banquet of life.

Instead of thoroughly enjoying the banquet, we become upset that the meal will not last forever. We criticize the food. We want one food and not another. Or, we gorge ourselves w ith w rong food for our system and then wonder why we become ill.

Many people spend their entire time at the feast looking for faults in the other guests. They have no idea at all who their host is, or why they have been invited in the first place. Most of the time they never think of offering thanks.

Some do not care at all about what they are doing at this enormous feast. When the food runs out, they simply feel terrified. Others don't care so much about the food, they just want to push the other guests around. They are under the illusion that this is their party and do not yet realize that all have been invited here to partake equally in the feast.

Some refuse to eat the meal entirely and go to the corner to pout, waiting for the party to end.

Prayer is a way of looking for the host, offering thanks and beginning to discover why we have been invited here. Prayer says "thank you," eats its fill and then asks, "What can I offer in return?"

As we pray we discover that each person at this banquet is precious in who they are and has been invited here for a reason. There is something unique that each guest has to contribute, including ourselves.

When we are ill and in pain it may be difficult to turn our minds towards prayer for the first time. When prayer is included in our daily life, however, it becomes a natural response that we can easily call upon during difficult times.

Prayer is also a way of remembering that one day we will be departing. It helps us be conscious and loving of others who are in the same position as we are.

There are many different ways of praying and of

attaining this state of being. Although it may be helpful, we do not necessarily always have to pray at designated places, at designated times.

Work may become a form of prayer when it is done in this state of mindful reverence, and dedicated to the good of all. A physician with a patient or a carpenter with a block of wood may both be engaged in the activity of prayer.

Bowing deeply (within and without) to one another, or to any aspect of life is another beautiful way to be praying. It is the vivid act of surrender, and honor. It is letting go of our self-centered opinions, desires, and all the demands we constantly make upon life.

PROCESS

Look at your child (or friend, lover, mate, whomever) and bow to him first thing in the morning. (If not on the outside, do it in your mind.)

Bow to this person before you offer him food. (See how you feel after you do this, both about them and yourself.)

Now, stop for a moment, pause, and bow to whomever you are in an interaction with. You are bowing and offering reverence for their life and for yours.

As we pray deeply, we gradually become empty and clean. We become one with the entire universe and lose our sense of being alone. As prayer deepens, we let go of the notion that we are so special, better than the other, and that the entire world revolves around us. Instead we begin to allow ourselves to be truly instructed. This is an invocation of the highest and best we are capable of.

A life and practice of continuing prayer (in any form) is the best possible preparation to greet illness, pain or any kind of loss. It is also the best possible instruction to live most fully with the greatest understanding and joy.

All that we are, all that we need and know is already deep within. When we engage in true prayer, our inner treasure house is lovingly opened.

ABOUT THE AUTHOR

Brenda Shoshanna Lukeman, Ph.D., psychologist and psychotherapist, has worked with the seriously ill, their families and staff for eighteen years.

Author, playwright, and long term Zen student, her work includes and integrates all different aspects of the journeys we take from suffering to health.

She has given workshops and seminars both regionally and nationally, and has taught both philosophy and psychology at Adelphi University and at the New Seminary. Presently she teaches psychology and Zen at the Zen Studies Society, NYC.

Workshops, consultations and seminars are available.

Order Form

☎ Telephone Orders: Call Toll Free: 1-800-879-4214
(Bookcrafters Distributors). Most major credit cards accepted.

▭ Postal Orders:
Steppingstones Press
P.O. Box 220-249
Great Neck, NY 11022

Please send me _____ copies of:
Journey Through Illness & Beyond

Company Name:_____

Name:_____

Address:_____

City:_____State_____Zip_____-____

Sales Tax
Please add 8.5% sales tax for books shipped to NY addresses

Shipping & Handling
Book Rate: $3 for the first book abd 75 cents for each
additional book
(Surface shipping may take three to four weeks)
Air Mail: $4 per book

Payment
☐ Check
☐ Money Order

Call *Toll Free* and Order Now!
1-800-879-4214